NOW YOU CAN SPEED-READ—WITHOUT TEARS!

SUPER READING SECRETS is a revolutionary, easily applied speed-reading technique. Whether you are a professional, a student, or a book lover, you'll be surprised at how much fun you'll have learning how to super read. This complete guide includes:

- guided exercises for mastering speed and comprehension
- self-testing drills
- hands-on techniques for practicing
- tips for slow readers and those for whom English is a second language
- appendices of essential information.

All this—and more—will help you tap your mind's hidden potential and reach reading levels you never thought possible...in the classroom, on the job, and in your life.

★ ★ ★

SUPER READING SECRETS

HOWARD STEPHEN BERG

WARNER BOOKS

NEW YORK   BOSTON

WARNER BOOKS EDITION

Cover design by Don Puckey

Warner Books, Inc.
1271 Avenue of the Americas
New York, NY 10020

Visit our Web site at
www.warnerbooks.com

A Time Warner Company

Printed in the United States of America

First Printing: September, 1992

15   14

Dedicated to the memory of my mother,
who didn't live to see the seed
that she sowed flower.

Contents

<u>INTRODUCTION</u>

While walking in a crowded mall you suddenly spot a familiar face; one you haven't seen in years. Yet, you instantly recognize it as belonging to a friend who you have wanted to contact for a long time. How is it that a mind that distinguishes a face that appears unexpectedly in a large congregation of people reads one word at a time in a book? The fact is that you do not have to read this way. You can change the way your mind reads so that you can use the same visual power you exercise in every other life activity.

Once properly trained, your mind can identify large groups of words with the same unconscious effort used to spot objects in your day-to-day life. The brain is like a wonderful computer, capable of visually processing huge amounts of data in an instant. All you need is a system that enables you to apply your full visual power to reading. *Super reading* is a system that will allow you to accomplish this task. Using the techniques described in this book, you will soon be reading phrases, paragraphs, and even whole pages with as little effort as you now give to reading single words.

WHAT IS SUPER READING?

Super reading will provide you with a wide range of skills that will have you mastering information you once considered incomprehensible. By using super reading, you will be able to:

- reach you maximal reading speed
- increase your comprehension of text
- memorize quickly large amounts of information
- master study skills
- concentrate and maximize your mental power

Reaching Maximal Reading Speed

Maximal reading speed can be achieved in two ways. Most speed-reading courses usually rely upon drills that develop your mechanical skills to increase your reading speed. These drills train your eye to scan text at high rates. Mechanical skills of this type are called *motor skills* by psychologists. All motor skills involve learning to co-ordinate physical activity with a task. You are already familiar with a large number of motor skills which may include typing, driving a car, playing an instrument, performing in sports, and dancing. The key to mastering motor skills is frequent practice on a regular basis. This is more important than attempting to cram all your study into a single practice session each week. Mastering speed-reading motor skills is best accomplished by brief daily exercises rather than studying several hours on a weekend. No doubt there will be days when you will be unable to find even a brief moment for practice. This is of no consequence unless it becomes your pattern. Just like learning an instrument, the more regularly you practice, the sooner you will master super reading.

Unlike most speed-reading programs, super reading does not rely solely upon motor skills to increase your speed. Instead, it uses the latest breakthroughs in psychology in teaching people how to read more intelligently. The area of psychological research that deals with how the mind learns is called *metacognitive psychology*. By using metacognitive techniques, you will increase your reading speed even without practicing your motor skills. However, using both motor skills and metacognitive techniques at the same time will produce reading speeds greater than either method produces on its own.

Increasing Comprehension of Text

No matter how quickly you read, nothing of value is accomplished without understanding. Many reading professors now believe that the single most important factor used to understand text is schema. *Schema* is a term describing all the information you already possess when learning something new. Super reading is crammed with tips on using schema to master details even when you find a book confusing.

Developing a Powerful Memory

Isn't it strange that you can remember the words to songs on the radio simply by hearing one or two notes from an instrument? This is even stranger when you consider that you probably have never read the lyrics. Yet the memory of these songs persists in your mind for years. One twang on the bass guitar and you remember the lyrics to one of a hundred Beatles' songs; yet, a book you read last night can be difficult to remember. Wouldn't it be wonderful if you could learn to remember things you read as effortlessly as you remember the words to songs you hear? You can. Chapter Seven, How To Develop A Super Memory, is crammed with techniques that will help you memorize even complex information with a minimum of effort.

Mastering Study Skills

You've just spent days studying for that important meeting or exam. Confidently, you prepare to answer the questions and then it happens. Question after question is asked that you know nothing about. Performing poorly when you fail to properly prepare might be expected, but failing after diligent studying is an undeserved frustration. Is there anything you can do to avoid this situation? The section on Mastering Study Skills describes how to determine what questions are most likely to be asked of you before you begin to study. It even describes how to use far less time to master information.

Increasing Concentration

You are about to learn how to read a page in only three seconds. At this speed even a brief distraction can result in missing important details. Nonetheless, the world will not come to a silent halt while your mind is focusing upon information you want to learn. Learning to concentrate is a skill that will enable you to tune out the annoying distractions around you. The screeching horns, the noisy children, and countless other distractions will no longer draw your focus away from your reading.

Environmental conditions aren't the only distractions that can interfere with learning at high speeds. Negative emotions like depression, anxiety, and fear exert a detrimental influence on your ability to comprehend and retain information. Fortunately there is a solution to all these problems. For centuries, those with the most advanced minds have developed their mental powers by mastering meditative techniques. Super reading will provide you with several different meditation exercises that will enable you to develop a well-focused mind that can comprehend information at high speeds.

PREPARING TO MASTER SUPER READING

Today's harried lifestyle leaves precious little time for undertaking new projects. One of the nicest things about super reading is how little time it requires from you to learn its secrets. In as little as 16 to 30 minutes a day, over an eight-week period, you will develop skills that will last a lifetime. This modest investment in time will be repaid repeatedly as you become a faster and a more efficient reader. Still, you must be willing to practice the minimum time suggested in order to derive the full benefit from this program. If not, your reading skills will improve, but not thoroughly.

WHAT ABOUT SLOW AND BILINGUAL READERS?

It may seem ludicrous to say that you must be able to read before you learn to speed read. Yet, I've given workshops where individuals reading five to six words per minute expected to increase their speeds to thousands of words per minute. If you read slower than 100 words per minute, you should first consider taking a program in remedial reading before attempting to master super-reading skills. Still, much of the material in this book will help even the slowest readers to sharpen their reading competence. Having normal reading ability will help ensure the type of results you seek from this program. Often, bilingual students attend super-reading workshops with mixed results. Those who read and think fluently in English are more successful than those who must translate what they read into their native tongue. While the extra step of translation bars access to the highest reading speed, it will not prevent bilingual students from reading, comprehending, and learning faster.

THE SECRET OF SUPER-FAST READING

When reading over 60 pages per minute, an altered state of consciousness is experienced. The text seems to disappear as you become one with the book. You actually read faster than your mind can think. In this heightened state, text appears as images and experiences rather than words and phrases. It almost seems as though you are viewing a movie instead of reading a book. This oneness of mind and text is the Zen method of reading. It is the result of integrating meditation techniques with the other super-reading methods outlined in this book. Discipline and practice must be maintained over a long period of time to reach these extremely high reading speeds. Yet with persistence, your efforts will be rewarded as you start to complete in minutes the same amount of text that once took hours.

WHY DO *YOU* READ?

Enjoyment, self-development, and understanding are the three reasons most of us read. To make the most productive use of your time, always be aware of why you are reading a text. As you learn super reading, you will find many techniques available to make you a master reader. You will learn to vary these techniques to fit your particular reading purpose. Feel free to experiment with these techniques. Develop a super-reading style in harmony with both your purpose and how your mind functions. These skills are meant to be controlled by you. You should not be controlled by them. Avoid becoming distressed or tense if you encounter some frustration in your early attempts. Unlearning your old reading style requires practice and patience. The most important thing to remember when practicing your super-reading skills is to avoid placing mental pressure on yourself. Relax and enjoy the power of super reading.

CHAPTER ONE

How the Mind Decodes Text

GOALS

- UNDERSTANDING HOW THE MIND DECODES TEXT
- UNDERSTANDING THE THREE LEVELS OF TEXTUAL MEANING
- UNDERSTANDING HOW SCHEMA DETERMINES TEXTUAL MEANING

JUMPING FROM WORDS TO PHRASES

Shiny ornaments and Santa decorations hang in every store window as you briskly make your way through the crowded mall. Passing a leather goods store, your eyes glance down, glimpsing a designer wallet you've wanted for the past few months. Turning to enter the store, you spot Bob, an old friend you haven't seen in years. Isn't it amazing how much detail your eyes can instantly analyze in your daily life? Details that you use to make quick decisions. It's even more amazing when you realize that you use these same eyes to read only one word at a time in text. Something is definitely wrong with how you read, and the problem began during childhood.

As a child, you were taught to read letters that formed units called words. Watch a child read a word like *dog* as if it were three distinct letters, d-o-g. When was the last time you were conscious of letters in text? Can you imagine reading a book and saying, "Great book, lots of interesting letters. I loved all the words containing *p*'s, *q*'s and *z*'s." It would be ridiculous. As an adult, you read words without an awareness of the letters they contain. Just as most adults read words without being conscious of letters, it is possible for you to decode entire passages at a glance without an awareness of words. The only reason you can't read entire passages speedily is because our school system doesn't teach you to read beyond the single-word unit.

Look at the words *hot dog*. They are two distinct words that your brain perceives as a single unit. Just as your mind can integrate these two words into a single meaning, it can also interpret a sentence, paragraph, or even an entire page. All it takes is a system to accomplish this feat. Super reading is the perfect system for comprehending numerous words at a glance.

WRITING IS CRYSTALLIZED THOUGHT

Reading is the decoding of symbols into meaning. Before learning to read fast, it's important to have an appreciation for writing's significance. Writing is nothing more than speech represented by printed symbols. Once, writing was the sole domain of priests; it was a sacrilege for a layman to know how to read or write. A magical power was seen in the written word. To these ancient holy men, writing represented crystallized thought, someone's understanding captured on a document. Even today, in the Jewish religion, prayer books are not discarded when old; instead they are placed in coffins with the deceased and buried as if they were a living thing that had died. Super reading recognizes that as a reader you are learning to decode thoughts placed on paper. Focusing upon the meanings created by the text frees you from dependency upon each individual word, resulting in larger chunks of information being read at a time with a commensurate increase in both speed and comprehension of text.

THE THREE LEVELS OF TEXTUAL MEANING

Text can contain three levels of meaning: literal, implied, and inferential. All three levels can occur within the same written document.

Literal information includes everything specifically stated in a written document. Names, dates, and formulas are common examples of literal information. In many cases, literal information needs to be memorized so it can be accurately recalled.

Implied information is not specifically stated. It contains facts that must be analyzed using information commonly possessed by an average reader. For example, an author might describe a woman in a scarlet dress, but wouldn't tell you that scarlet is a shade of red. The author expects you to recognize scarlet as a shade of red.

Inferential reading requires you to scrutinize text as an expert. You question, probe, and challenge the opinions and statements of an author. Inferential information is often quite difficult for a reader to decode because it requires considerable experience with a subject. Unlike the common experiences needed to read text at the implied level, inferential information is rarely known by average individuals; instead, it is usually possessed by professionals in a field. Imagine attempting to critically read a technical report on the biochemical effects of a new medication without any background in chemistry or medicine. Without this background you simply could not assess the validity of the article. This type of critical reading is representative of inferential reading. Most people can only read inferentially in subjects related to their work or serious interests.

HOW SCHEMA DETERMINES TEXTUAL MEANING

One of the most important things you can use to decode text is schema. Schema is the information you already possess when learning something new. Although you unconsciously possess this information, you constantly use it when decoding text. Often, schema is acquired so early in life we don't even remember obtaining it.

Surgical breakthroughs which enable people blind since birth to see during adulthood provided psychologists with an opportunity to test the importance of schema obtained during early childhood. Amazingly, many individuals seeing for the first time in adulthood required up to six months to learn to distinguish between a square and a circle. This task is easy for you because your schema of shape discrimination developed while you were lying on your back in a crib watching different shapes passing in front of your eyes. Throughout life we develop schema. Each of us possesses a unique schema that shapes our reactions to and understanding of life events. For example, when you tell someone, "I love you," prior experiences with love affect the reaction to your words.

Schema is the backbone of super reading. Properly used, it enables you to read at high speeds with excellent comprehension. Let's perform an exercise that highlights both the importance of schema, and the three levels of meaning contained within text.

Exercise

Imagine for a moment I have the power to turn you into a four-year-old child attending preschool just prior to Columbus Day. You've never heard of Christopher Columbus, and I'm about to enlighten you about the importance of tomorrow's holiday.

"The year is 1492, and a man named Christopher Columbus just crossed the ocean from Europe and discovered America. I'd like you children to answer some questions about what I just discussed. First, who can tell me the name of the man who crossed the Atlantic Ocean in 1492?"

"Christopher Columbus," you proudly respond.

You knew the answer because I provided you with the

specific information. This is an example of literal information acquired from text—information that is given.

"Who can tell me how Columbus traveled to America?"

"He took a boat," you logically respond.

But wait—how did you know he took a boat? I didn't say anything about Columbus taking a boat, all I mentioned was that he crossed the ocean separating Europe from America. If you were going to travel to Europe today, you'd probably take a plane. So why didn't you suggest that Columbus took a plane? Using schema, you knew planes didn't exist in 1492; the only logical method of traveling across the ocean during this time period was a boat. Most adult Americans know that boats were used to cross the ocean in the year 1492, making this an excellent example of an implied meaning in text. If only a small segment of the population knew this information, then this would be an example of inferential reading.

When you think about it, even the concept of a boat is subject to interpretation. Many children might envision the *Love Boat* as the means of transportation. A *Love Boat* with people strolling the decks, drinking glasses donning little umbrellas, and all the comforts of home. How many young children would envision a tiny wooden craft similar to the one that actually took Columbus to the New World? It would be even more difficult to explain what a ship and an ocean were to a child who had been born in a desert and had never seen the sea. Schema can both help and hurt our understanding of text.

No author would attempt to provide all the schema necessary for reading a book. Can you imagine having to explain in a history book that planes weren't used by Columbus because internal combustion engines hadn't been invented? The amount of information that an author would need to provide would become an unmanageable task. All authors have to assume their readers possess some background. When an author makes the wrong assumptions, a book becomes difficult to read.

"Last question, children. What made Columbus take his famous trip that resulted in his discovery of America?"

It would take a pretty precocious four-year-old to determine that Columbus was searching for a new trade route to the East to avoid the hazard of encountering barbarians. Actually, no one could answer this question without additional information about the time period in which Columbus lived. Inferential questions are of this nature, requiring detailed information for accurate conclusions to be made.

Schema and Reading Difficulties

Have you ever found it difficult to understand a book that others seem to easily comprehend? The difficulty may lie with the writer rather than with you. If an author fails to provide necessary schema, comprehending the text becomes difficult. Usually, this occurs when an author erroneously assumes you possess a schematic background in the subject, a background that others obtained by reading other books or through various life experiences. This type of problem is often encountered in academic writing. Authors, particularly those who have spent their lives immersed in a technical subject, often become desensitized to the complexity of their material and assume everyone will find their information easy to follow. Naturally, those having the assumed background or schema can effortlessly read the same material that would be challenging to you.

Although *schema* is a single word, it usually means a conglomeration of information about a topic. Schema enables you to read materials at higher speeds because you recognize the familiar ideas encoded by text, rather than the individual words. Even if you miss a few words when speed reading, it is unlikely you will miss a familiar concept which permeates long passages of text. We shall learn in later chapters how to master material for which we have little schema.

Possessing schema in a subject enables you to read even difficult material with ease. Schema is the reason a biologist can read a biology book faster than an art book. The technical terms and concepts of biology are part of a biologist's everyday life, but the information in the art book is unfamiliar. Similarly, an artist, possessing schema about art, would find an art book easier to read than a biology book.

To illustrate how dependent you are upon schema when reading text, I've composed a passage in which schema has been deliberately removed. Although this passage is about something you know, the lack of schema will make it difficult for you to comprehend. Take a moment now to try and comprehend the following exercise.

Exercise

This is an easy thing to do. If possible, you will do it at home, but you can always go somewhere else if it is necessary. Beware of doing too much at once. This is a major mistake and may cost you quite a bit of money. It is far better to do too little than attempt to do too much. Make sure everything is grouped properly. Put everything into its appropriate place. Now you are ready to proceed. The next step is to put things into another convenient arrangement. Once done, you'll probably have to start again really soon. Most likely, you'll be doing this for the rest of your life—perhaps not. Who knows?

OK, can you tell me what this passage describes? Did I hear you say laundry? If you did, then you're correct. Notice that this selection omits all references to clothing, detergent, washing machine, dryer, laundromat, or any other information you might use as a schematic clue. The difficulty you experienced when trying to read this passage is identical to the problem you have when reading text lacking critical schematic information. It is difficult to identify the subject without this important information.

Take another look at this exercise. It would have been easy for you to read and comprehend this passage if the title *Laundry* appeared centered right above it. Sometimes all it takes is a single word to provide the schema you need to understand a passage. Fortunately, most authors—with the exception of some lawyers—do not intentionally strip the schema from their text as I just did. A typical author attempts to provide the schema you will need to understand the writing. Consequently, you must search for the schematic clues offered by an author when you experience difficulty while reading. Usually, you can find a critical word or phrase that will help you understand the writing. If you experience difficulty interpreting a book's schema, you will find several chapters in this book that offer useful tips on how to find and use a book's schema.

Just as a lack of schema can make understanding text difficult, passages rich in schema are easy to comprehend. In the exercise found below, I've written a story that lacks sentences, grammar, paragraphs, and all the elements of writing usually considered essential. The passage consists of nothing more than a checkbook register with dated entries, amounts, and the name of the individual writing the checks. Yet, because it is rich in schema, you will be able to read this selection with a great deal of understanding.

Exercise

8/1/02	Medical Center	$500.00	Bob Clarke
8/2/02	Abe's Baby Furniture	$280.00	Bob Clarke
9/2/02	Dr. Peterson	$300.00	Bob Clarke, Sr.
12/12/02	Celia's Toy Store	$91.75	Bob Clarke, Sr.
8/30/09	St. John's Boy's Prep.	$3,000.00	Bob Clarke, Sr.
8/30/14	Hamilton Military Academy	$3,500.00	Bob Clarke, Sr.
9/1/20	Fred's Cadillac	$4,200.00	Bob Clarke, Sr.
9/8/20	Sam's Body Shop	$400.00	Bob Clarke, Sr.

Let's examine the information contained within this unusual passage on the literal level. Obviously, this is a story about a man named Bob Clarke. Bob becomes the father of a baby son sometime around August 1. When old enough, the boy is sent to prep school, and later to a military academy. Sometime around the boy's eighteenth birthday, Bob purchases a new Cadillac which requires body work four days later. Bob's checkbook specifically states all these facts.

Reading this passage on the implied level adds an additional level of meaning. Although the exact date of birth is not given, we can determine the baby most likely was born either on the first or second day in August. There are two pieces of evidence indicating these are the likely birth dates. First, the hospital receives payment on August 1, the date the mother was probably admitted to the hospital. Second, Dr. Peterson receives payment on September 2, approximately thirty days after services were rendered. There certainly appears to be quite a bit of evidence supporting our hypothesis on the date of birth. Additional information can be gleaned by reading on the implied level of this passage. Most likely, the baby is named Bob Clarke, *Jr.* as indicated by the addition of *Sr.* to his father's name.

More subtle information is also revealed on the implied level of this passage. You can determine Bob's economic condition from the information it contains. Bob appears to be quite wealthy as indicated by the $91.75 spent on toys on December 12, 1902. When I showed this figure to Alex, my ten-year-old son, he thought Bob was really cheap in spending so little on a Christmas present. Alex doesn't have the schema we possess about the value of money during the early part of this century. Schema that indicates that a huge amount of money was spent on the toys. Even if you weren't certain about the value of this money, the passage contains additional information useful in evaluating the value of a dollar in 1902. We contrast the $91.75 spent on toys in 1902 with the cost of a new Cadillac 18 years later for only $4,200.

Imagine buying a new Cadillac today for that sum of money! A simple analysis of these figures proves beyond any doubt that $91.75 was a considerable sum of money to spend on toys in 1902.

During my super-reading workshops, I ask everyone to determine the type of relationship Bob Clarke, Sr. had with his son. Using the inferential level of meaning contained in this passage, two distinct interpretations are given. Many individuals describe Bob Clarke, Sr. as a man of wealth and power whose desire for privacy motivated him to send his son to boarding school and military school. Certainly, this is a scenario supported by the information contained within the passage. Others dispute this interpretation. They believe that Bob wanted his son to develop into a disciplined gentleman, capable of responsibility handling the money and power his father would one day hand on to him. Both versions could be supported by the data contained in this passage, which raises an important point about inferential meanings. Often, inferential information is neither true nor false; your reaction to the information is affected by your prior experiences in life.

Take a moment and examine the bill from Sam's Body Shop on September 8. When I ask students in my super-reading workshop to explain the cause of this bill, the majority usually believe that Bob Clarke, Jr. had an accident. One which made it necessary for his father to fix his car. Others believe that the new car had a defect when purchased which required making a repair not covered by a warranty offered in 1920. Upon questioning the students having this second opinion, I discovered the majority had experienced problems with new cars they had purchased, and that this had altered their schema and affected their interpretation of the passage.

Exercise

In a nonfiction book on a subject you have never read about before, read a few chapters and interpret their meanings on the literal, implied, and inferential levels. Repeat the exercise using a nonfiction book on a familiar subject. Make an effort to be conscious of how your mind interacts with the material in both books. Notice how you use schema to easily master the familiar material, and pay attention to how your lack of schema creates a learning problem. Begin to look for the schematic clues offered by an author that will help you master difficult material with less effort.

Summary

1. Children learn to read letters.
2. Adult readers interpret the meanings of words.
3. Super readers focus upon the meanings of passages.
4. The information we possess when learning something new is called *schema*.
5. Schema enables you to maintain comprehension when reading at high speeds.
6. Text contains three levels of meaning.
7. Literal meanings are specifically stated in text.
8. Implied meanings can easily be decoded using schema.
9. Inferential meanings of text require extensive background to be interpreted.

CHAPTER TWO

How to Increase Your Reading Speed

- DETERMINING YOUR INITIAL READING RATE
- MEASURING YOUR READING RATE IN ANY TEXT
- DEVELOPING TECHNIQUES FOR CO-ORDINATING YOUR HAND AND EYE MOTIONS
- INCREASING YOUR READING SPEED BY USING SPEED MASTERY TECHNIQUES

Most speed-reading systems rely primarily upon mechanical skills to increase your reading rate. Learning a mechanical technique requires mastering a motor skill. Motor skills you probably already know include typing, playing an instrument, driving a car, and performing in sports activities like swimming. Mastering motor skills requires frequent sessions with repetitive practice. For example, learning to type requires hitting each key hundreds of times until your fingers instinctively hit each key.

Since reading is a habit learned early in life, it usually takes considerable practice to replace your old reading method using mechanical techniques. Most speed-reading systems require practicing for at least a month. Often they require from 30 to 60 minutes of daily training to achieve a higher reading speed. After instructing hundreds of speed-reading workshops, I know that most speed-reading students lack the time these programs require.

Many people who rely primarily upon mechanical methods experience another serious problem. They lose their higher reading speed unless they continually read at their optimum rate. At times, everyone prefers to read slowly, making sole dependency upon mechanical methods unacceptable. Fortunately, the super-reading system enables you to get the benefits of mechanical techniques for increasing reading speed, while eliminating their potential hazards.

Traditional mechanical skills are only part of the super-reading system. Super reading uses many metacognitive techniques for increasing your reading rate. Metacognition is the branch of psychology that deals with questions concerning how the brain masters learning. Super reading describes how your mind decodes text. This enables you to adjust your reading speed for different materials without losing your peak speed. Since super reading does not depend solely upon motor skills, you will increase your reading speed in hours instead of days.

DETERMINING YOUR INITIAL READING RATE

In any self-development program, you must measure your initial skill level. Before learning to increase your reading rate, you must calculate your current reading speed. As your reading speed increases, you can refer to this initial rate to determine your progress.

Use the passage immediately following this section to determine your current reading rate. There are about ten words on each numbered line. Use the following steps to determine your reading speed:

1. Set an alarm so that it rings one minute from your starting point.
2. When it rings, stop reading, and look at the line's number listed in the right column.
3. Multiply this number by ten (the average number of words per line) to find your initial reading speed.

EXAMPLE

Imagine that after reading for one minute you are on line 30 in the sample text. Multiplying 30 by 10 gives you an initial reading speed of 300 words per minute.

1	**Reality—What a Concept!**
2	Even as you read, a revolution is occurring in the
3	minds of scientists. A revolution that will affect every-
4	thing that touches your life. Yet this is a strange revolu-
5	tion. No explosions, no guns, not even a glimmer of activi-
6	ty that might reveal its presence. This is not a violent
7	revolution with maimings and death; instead, it is about how
8	science views reality. The consequences of this incredible

9   vision are only beginning to affect your life.

10   Quantum physics has opened a crack into the mystery of
11   the creation of the universe itself. A crack that sharp-
12   minded scientists are trying to widen each day. For the
13   layman, their discoveries are almost unkown. Some cryptic
14   puzzle of math and physics that many erroneously believe is not
15   meant for the minds of ordinary men. Yet the effects of
16   these discoveries threaten to dwarf even the significance of
17   nuclear energy. Discoveries that will not only change the
18   way you live, but alter the way you think about reality. As
19   the world's fastest reader, I used my skill to investigate
20   the wonderful discoveries these brilliant men have made. As
21   you sharpen your reading speed using my writing samples, I
22   will provide you with information that reveals some of these
23   incredible discoveries. You will find this information
24   given in a down-to-earth fashion that will not cloud the
25   importance of this work with technical formulas and equa-
26   tions that often do more to confuse than to inform.

THE PHILOSOPHICAL ROOTS

28   Till the start of the 20th century, Western civiliza-
29   tion has been founded upon a very simple form of logic. A
30   system of logic begun by the Greek philosopher Aristotle.
31   Under this logic system something either exists or it
32   doesn't. This may seem simple in concept, but the new
33   physics requires a completely different form of logic. For
34   example, everyone knows that something is either alive or
35   dead. Since these terms contradict each other, both state-
36   ments cannot be true at the same time—can they? Biologists
37   have discovered that a virus exists as a nonliving crystal
38   while outside a body, but immediately exhibits all the
39   characteristics of a living organism once inside a host.
40   Remove it from the host's body, and once again it appears to

41 be nonliving. Is it living or nonliving? The answer to
42 this question is no. The answer is also yes!
43   The 20th century ushered in a new type of logic. A
44 logic that permits things to exist in complete contradiction.
45 The logic of relativity in which truth is
46 based on how you perceive an event. For example, imagine I am
47 in a room with a woman. I can see that she is an individu-
48 al, and I am an individual. Yet I also can see us as a
49 couple. Both statements are true, and also both statements
50 are false. The truthfulness and falseness of these state-
51 ments depends upon how I look at the relationship between
52 myself and this woman. This ability for something to con-
53 tradict itself, and yet for both parts of the contradiction
54 to be simultaneously true, lies at the center of the new
55 quantum physics. A physics that routinely views contradic-
56 tions in nature as being both logical and true.

57   **The Mystery of Light**

58   Possibly nothing in physics has stirred more controver-
59 sy than the structure of light. Study light using one set
60 of conditions and it appears to be a wave. Study it using a
61 different set of conditions and it seems to be a solid
62 particle. So is light a wave or a particle? Both answers
63 appear to be correct. At first, this answer may not appear
64 extraordinary, but upon closer examination this response
65 becomes astonishing.

66   Waves and particles are in complete conflict with each
67 other. Until quantum theory, it was considered impossible
68 for anything to possess the attributes of both the wave and
69 particle at the same time. Particles have a definite loca-
70 tion in time and space. Importantly, particles have mass or
71 weight. A particle is like a marble, but much smaller. If
72 someone hit you with a marble traveling at a very high speed it would

73 hurt. Waves are completely different from particles. Waves
74 lack a specific location, and they do not have any mass. Yet
75 light appears to have the properties of both waves and
76 particles when viewed under different conditions. Let's
77 examine an experiment that demonstrates this unusual nature
78 of light.
79   Imagine shining a bright light onto a piece of card-
80 board that is sitting in front of a screen. If the cardboard
81 lacks a hole in it, then only the shadow of the cardboard
82 would appear on the screen. What do you think would
83 happen if you poked a very small hole into the center of the
84 cardboard? Scientists performed this experiment, and to no
85 one's surprise, the screen now had a patch of light upon it.
86 The light appeared to act like a particle or bullet. After
87 passing through the hole in the cardboard, it struck the
88 screen and spread a path of brightness as if it were a shattered
89 particle. Under these conditions, light definitely appears
90 to be a particle.
91   What do you think would happen if you poked a second
92 tiny hole into the cardboard near the first one? Logically,
93 you might expect the path of brightness behind the card-
94 board to be twice as bright. After all, you now have two
95 holes permitting the light to shine onto the screen. This
96 is not what happens. Instead, gazing at the screen, your
97 eyes would view a series of circles identical to the ones
98 you would see in a pond after a rock was thrown into it.
99 This circular pattern is well known to physicists as the
100 fingerprint of a wave pattern. Viewed in this fashion, light
101 definitely seems to be a wave pattern. How could this
102 possibly happen? How could something as simple as punching
103 a hole in a piece of cardboard change the appearance of
104 light from that of a solid particle into a massless wave?

105   Quantum theory contains these incredible paradoxes that are
106   only now starting to be understood. We shall continue our
107   investigation of this wondrous science in the next reading
108   selection.
109
110   WRITE DOWN YOUR STARTING READING SPEED
      HERE:_____

MEASURING YOUR READING RATE
IN ANY TEXT

It is safe to say that the lines in most of the texts you
read are not numbered. You should be able to determine
your reading rate in different books to estimate your
completion time, and also for measuring your reading
progress. Naturally, your aptitude in a subject will affect
your reading speed; so, you will find your speed will
vary in different books. To determine your reading rate,
follow the steps shown below:

1. Set an alarm clock so that it rings after one minute.
2. Read at your comprehension rate until the alarm rings.
3. Count the number of words in five typical lines. Be
   careful to count lines and not sentences. Do not count
   punctuation marks as words.
4. Round off the number of words to the nearest number
   divisible by five.
5. Divide your total by five, and write down your answer. This will give you the average number of words per
   line.
6. Count the number of lines on a typical page. Write
   down this number.

7. Multiply the number of words on an average line b the average number of lines per page. This will give yo the average number of words per page.
8. Divide this number by four to determine the averag number of words on a quarter page.
9. Measure the amount you read to the nearest quarte page, and multiply by the number of words per page.

EXAMPLE OF MEASURING YOUR BASIC READING RATE IN ANY TEXT

1. After reading for one minute, you find 56 words on five typical lines.
2. You round off 56 to 55, the nearest number divisible by 5.
3. Dividing 50 by 5 produces 10 as the average number of words per line.
4. The page has 40 lines.
5. You multiply 40 lines per page by 10 words per average line and find it equals 400 words on a typical page.
6. You read a page and a half in one minute. 400 words per page multiplied by 1.5 pages equals 600 words per minute.

IMPORTANT

Do not use the first page in a chapter to determine the typical number of words per page. In many books, this page contains blank space to set off the chapter title from the rest of the text. Consequently, the number of lines on a chapter's first page is usually far less than the number of lines on a typical page.

Normal Reading Rate

Super reading works for anyone having normal reading ability. The normal reading rate is between 150 and 400 words per minute. Most likely, your initial speed falls within this range. If your speed is far less than 100 words per minute, you may require remedial-reading training. Although students reading as slowly as 80 words per minute have reported success with super-reading techniques. Naturally, you get the best results when your starting rate is within the normal range.

Students unable to read fluently in a language also will experience trouble with high-speed reading. You must read a language fluently before you can read it at high speed. I gave a workshop in San Francisco that was attended by a young German gentleman who spoke English. This young man used a German text to practice the super-reading skills that he had learned in English. He achieved excellent results using a book printed in his native language. If you can read fluently in other languages, then you will also be able to use your super-reading skills in these languages. Translating unfamiliar words and phrases is an extra step that will slow down your reading rate in a language unfamiliar to you.

PREPARING TO INCREASE SPEED

When a symphonic orchestra plays, one figure attracts the most attention from the audience—the conductor. Yet the conductor does not even play an instrument. Standing in front of the ensemble, his baton co-ordinates the actions of all the musicians.

During speed reading, your hand co-ordinates your eye movements, just as the conductor's baton keeps the musicians in an orchestra in harmony with each other. Learning to link your eye motion to your hand motion is the first step in preparing to increase your reading speed. Although different hand motions are described in various speed-reading books, they all have several common purposes.

The Purposes of Hand Motions

1. Your hand forces your eyes to scan text from one margin to the other, preventing any important words from being missed.

Some speed-reading systems use a hand motion that does not move the eye from one side of the text to the other. Instead, they suggest moving the eye straight down the center of the page. I do not recommend using this technique unless you are reading text containing very narrow columns. In regular text, most students find using this technique results in their eyes missing important phrases.

2. Your hand forces your eyes to continually scan new text. This prevents your eyes from stopping to look at unfamiliar phrases or words.

A common cause of slow reading is the tendency for the eyes to stop or repeatedly stare at an unfamiliar phrase. If you find some unfamiliar words when reading at high speeds, your brain can usually determine the meaning of the text. In fact, you will probably find your comprehension improving, because at high speed you will find more schematic clues in the text that will diminish your comprehension problem.

3. Your hand forces your eyes to read at a speed exceeding your ability to hear words in your head. This enables you to read at your visual rather than your auditory rate.

As your reading rate increases, you will experience difficulty hearing the inner voice that previously helped you read. Many readers erroneously slow down their speed so that they can once again clearly hear their inner voices. Using your hand, you can force your eyes to scan text, even when your inner voice no longer can be understood. As a direct result of this action, ultimately, both your comprehension and speed will improve.

Common Problems of Speed Reading

When practicing skills for increasing your reading rate, you will briefly lose your reading comprehension. This makes perfect sense when you realize that your goal is to read faster than you can now comprehend. At some point you must read faster than you can understand. All readers learning to increase their reading rates experience this temporary comprehension loss, and it usually lasts no longer than 15 to 30 minutes. Achieving a higher reading rate while maintaining comprehension requires only a few minutes of faith in yourself. If you follow the instructions given in this text, and ignore any comprehension difficulty you temporarily experience, you will quickly find yourself reading with excellent understanding.

There is a second factor contributing to your brief loss of reading comprehension. The skills helping you to increase your reading speed are given in easy-to-follow components with each containing a fraction of the complete skill. Naturally, comprehension is impossible until you have the total skill. As you learn each part, you move closer to mastering the complete skill. Once all the parts are integrated, you will once again comprehend text, but at a much higher reading speed.

Much like learning to drive a car, hand motions are a motor skill that is only mastered through practice and repetition. The first time you hit the brakes in an auto, you feel like you're going through the window. On your first attempt to steer the car, the vehicle feels as if it might go off the road. A year later, you stop, steer, and drive without consciously controlling your hands and feet. With the passage of time, your driving skill becomes an automatic reaction, and so will your ability to speed read. The schematic and metacognitive skills offered in this book reduce to a fraction the amount of time normally needed for mastering hand motions. My experience in teaching speed reading shows that you obtain the best results if you first master the mechanical skills. Then you can derive the full benefits of the other methods.

Hand Motions for Increasing Speed

It seems we spend much of our adult life undoing damage that occurred during childhood. "Don't use your fingers while reading," said your grammar-school teacher. While mastering super reading, forget what your teacher told you about using your fingers. Using your hand to increase the rate at which your eyes view text will help you to quickly increase your reading speed.

If you spot pages in your text that are blank or contain pictures, continue reading the page as if it contained normal text. However, read it at a much higher speed than a page containing words. Speed reading is like running. Once you establish your pace, it is important to maintain it. In the time it takes to decide what to do about a blank or picture page, you could have completed the page and maintained your high speed-reading rate. **REMEMBER: MOVE YOUR HAND OVER BLANK AND PICTURE PAGES AS IF THEY CONTAINED TEXT.**

How to Move Your Fingers

Since you have two hands, you may wonder which one to use when speed reading. Most people find the left hand the logical choice for guiding the eyes through text. English text flows from left to right, and from the top to the bottom of a page. The left hand more efficiently follows this pattern than the right hand. Moreover, this leaves the right hand free for turning pages. Since pages in a text turn from right to left, this is the natural method to use: the left hand moving the eye, the right hand turning the pages. If you are extremely right-handed you might feel uneasy using the left hand. A natural feel to your hand motion is more important than using your left hand. So, if your right hand feels more natural than your left, then please use it.

During my seminars, students often ask me where their eyes should focus in relationship to their fingers. There are three possible places you can fix your eyes during reading:

1. Fix your eye on the left side of your fingers.
2. Fix your eye on the right side of your fingers.
3. Fix your eye directly above your fingers.

Experiment to discover which hand and focal points are most comfortable for you. In my workshop, I tell my students the one place you should not fix your eyes is upon your fingers. Unless you are reading a book on palmistry, this will serve no purpose. Seriously, do not get distracted by the motion of your fingers. Your fingers are simply pacing your eye motion through the text. With practice, your awareness of your fingers will soon fade. Still, the fingers' motion will continue to help you read faster than ever before.

Many books have tight bindings that make the pages snap shut. Always use your free hand to help keep the book from snapping shut while reading.

Turn to page 236 Appendix Two to determine the correct pattern for moving your hand forward through text.

Exercise

PICKING A HAND AND FOCAL POINT
(Use the Reading Selection in Appendix Two)

1. Begin this exercise using your left hand.
2. Set an alarm clock so that it rings after one minute.
3. Use your pointer finger and middle finger to move your eyes across the line of text.

4. During the first minute, fix your eyes behind your fingers.

5. During the second minute, fix your eyes in front of your fingers.

6. During the third minute, fix your eyes above your fingers.

7. For the next three minutes, repeat these steps using your right hand.

8. Decide which hand feels more comfortable, and where you want to focus your eyes.

9. Set an alarm clock so that it rings after five minutes.

10. Use your preferred hand and eye positions for five minutes, and continue practicing in Appendix Two.

11. Remember to use your free hand to keep the book from snapping shut.

Exercise

Learning to Turn Pages

On Cleveland's *Morning Exchange* television show I completed an 1,180-page book in under 20 minutes. Efficient page turning played an important role during this lengthy high-speed reading marathon. Learning to turn pages during high-speed reading is an important skill you too must learn.

Which method you use for turning depends upon the hand chosen to guide your eyes during reading. You will always turn pages using your right hand. Page turning will be slightly slower if you also use your right hand to guide your eyes across the lines of text. The difference between left- and right-hand page turning is not noticeable unless you read faster than 50 pages per minute. Most likely, this will not present a problem for you.

Comprehension is not important during the page-turning exercise. Focus solely upon the physical actions necessary for turning pages.

Left-Hand Page-Turning Technique Exercise

1. Use your left hand to start reading at the upper left-hand corner of this book's first page.
2. As your left hand begins to move down the page, slide your right hand under the corner of the top of the right page.
3. Grasp the edge of the right page, and wait until your left hand reaches the bottom of the right page.
4. Quickly flip over the page, and continue reading the next page with your left hand.
5. Remember to use your right hand to keep the text from snapping shut while reading.
6. Repeat steps 1 through 4 until you have completed ten pages.

Right-Hand Page-Turning Technique

1. Use your right hand to start reading at the upper left-hand corner of this book's first page.
2. When you reach the bottom of the left page, move your right hand to the top of the right page.
3. As you complete the right page, quickly slide your right hand up to the corner of the page and flip it over.

4. Remember to use your left hand to keep the text from snapping shut while reading.

Backward Reading

If you ever saw me reading on television, you noticed that I read text both forward and backward. Many speed-reading systems encourage students to master the art of backward reading. It is a more advanced technique, and is not for everyone. Actively reading in both directions is twice as fast as only reading forward. There is no wasted time when you read in both directions. Instead of a brief rest, the motion your hand makes while returning to the start of the next line is part of your active reading. This is similar to the action of a computer printer. A printer that prints in both directions is usually faster than one that does not.

When I first introduce backward reading at my workshops, students express severe doubt that it will work. They wonder how they can possibly comprehend text by reading in the reverse direction. I tell them, "The children reading Hebrew have no problem reading from left to right, nor do the children in China have difficulty reading text from the top to the bottom of the paper." Remember that reading is a habit learned early in life. You become accustomed to decoding the meaning of text in a particular direction due to habit. The human brain can decode words in any orientation that it is taught to use.

Let's try an experiment. Take a moment and look about the room by turning your head from left to right. Next, gaze at the same room but turn your head from right to left. Your eyes have no difficulty seeing the objects in a room regardless of what direction your head is moving. Your visual power works in either direction when viewing pictures, and after all, words are nothing more than pictures drawn from letters. It is only the habit of reading forward that prevents you from comprehending text in a backward direction.

Certain people are totally conditioned to reading forward, making backward reading difficult for them to use. It is far more important to be comfortable when reading at high speed than to read backward. After all, what will you gain from your increased speed if you only comprehend the meaning of every other line? Just relax if you find backward reading is not for you. This difficulty will not interfere with your forward speed-reading techniques.

In a moment, you will experiment with backward reading. If you find that you only comprehend text when reading forward, then stop reading backward until directed to do otherwise. Most people find that their brain reads text backward a bit differently from how it reads text forward. It helps to look for the verbs and nouns in a sentence when reading backward. The verbs are the action words in a sentence, while the nouns are the subject words. If your brain can pick out these key words, then you can probably read backward with good comprehension.

Ironically, it is easier to read backward if you read faster rather than slower. The brain is reading the pattern of the sentence, rather than the meanings of each word. Just as a Band-Aid hurts less when pulled off the skin quickly, so does the brain decode the meaning of text better at a higher speed. If you read too slowly, your awareness of each word will make backward reading painful. It also helps if you summarize and condense the meaning contained within the text, instead of trying to comprehend each word.

When reading backward your finger traces a pattern that looks similar to a winding stream. Here is a sample of that winding pattern.

I wrote these lines of text to illustrate the appearance of forward and backward reading. When you begin, you should place your fingers at the beginning of the line. Glide your fingers forward, and follow your fingers with your eyes. When you reach the end of the line, trace a slight curve with your fingers, and drop them down to the next line. Move your fingers back to the beginning of the next line as your eyes continue to follow your hand motion. Notice that when going in one direction your hand will appear to push your eyes, but while going in the other direction it will appear to pull your eyes along. This is quite natural. Initially, only read forward and backward one line at a time.

TIPS FOR BACKWARD READING

1. You can vary your reading speed by moving your hand faster or slower.
2. Tracing narrow loops through text gives the best comprehension, but slows down your reading speed.
3. Tracing wide loops through text gives the best reading speed, but can reduce the comprehension of text.
4. You can form both wide and narrow loops to get the optimum combination of speed and comprehension.
5. If you find it frustrating to read backward, discontinue

your efforts until you master forward reading at high speed.

HOW TO READ MORE LINES AT ONCE

When I was a college student, I spent my summers teaching swimming at various camps. Teaching swimming made me aware of how important it is to break down a complex skill like a swimming stroke into easy-to-learn steps. When I developed my super-reading program I remembered my swimming-instructor experience and broke down the super-reading technique into many easy-to-learn steps for mastering high-speed reading. Using the skills you have just mastered, you will now be able to read more than one line of text at a time.

Take a moment and look at a picture hanging on a wall. If there isn't a picture available, then look at one in a newspaper or magazine. Notice how your eyes not only see the whole picture, but also can focus upon parts of it. You will find it easier to see several lines of text at a time if you view the lines of text as pictures rather than writing.

Hold a book at arm's length from your eyes. Notice how you cannot see the words, but can view the shapes of the lines. When learning to read many lines at once, it is enough if you see lines the way they appeared when viewed from arm's length a moment ago. At this point, it is not necessary for you to comprehend text when trying to read more than one line at a time. It is important that you force your eyes to view larger sections of text as suggested in the next exercise.

Before starting the next exercise, I suggest you get a

blank cassette tape and a recorder. You should also use an alarm clock to perform this exercise. Superior results will be obtained using the script for tape that follows the exercise. Taping the instructions will enable you to continue your reading with a minimum of interruption.

Exercise

How to Read Multiple Lines of Text

1. Read Sample Unit Two, which starts on page 218.
2. Use an alarm clock to time your three-minute exercises.
3. Read one line of text at your best comprehension rate for three minutes.
4. Read two lines of text at a time for three minutes. For the duration of this exercise, it is not important that you comprehend the text.
5. Read four lines of text at a time for three minutes.
6. Read a paragraph at a time for three minutes.

SCRIPT FOR TAPE

Record the words on each numbered line onto a blank tape. Follow the instructions given in italics, but do not record them onto your tape.

1. "Start reading one line of text at your best comprehension rate."
   Wait for your alarm clock to ring after three minutes.
2. "Stop."
3. "Start reading two lines of text at a time."
   Wait for your alarm clock to ring after three minutes.

4. "Stop."
5. "Start reading four lines of text at a time."
   Wait for your alarm clock to ring after three minutes.
6. "Start reading a paragraph at a time."
7. "Stop."

How to Read at a Faster Rate

Reading several lines of text at once is not the only way to increase your reading rate. Increasing the speed of your hand motion also will increase your reading pace. As you begin increasing the motion of your hand, you will no longer comprehend text. This is of no importance! This is the brief period in super reading mentioned earlier that requires you to have faith in yourself. It is a challenge that I know you will now face and overcome.

Shortly, you will be given an activity requiring you to use your new ability to move swiftly through text. This exercise produces a beneficial effect upon your subconscious mind that enables you to read at high speed with comprehension. Move swiftly through this exercise so you can master the ability to scan text quickly. You are about to become a super-reading champion.

I recommend using a tape recorder when practicing the following exercise. You can continue using the tape from the previous exercises. A suggested script for tape follows the exercise.

Exercise

How to Read at a Faster Rate

1. Continue reading Sample Unit Two, which starts on page 218.
2. Use an alarm clock to time your three-minute exercises.
3. Complete one page every five seconds. Continue reading for three minutes. Make certain you complete each page in exactly five seconds. Do not concern yourself with comprehension during this exercise.
4. Complete one page every two seconds. Continue reading for three minutes.

SCRIPT FOR TAPE

Record the words on each numbered line onto a blank tape. Follow the instructions given in italics, but do not record them onto your tape.

1. "Start reading one page every five seconds."
   Wait for your alarm clock to ring after three minutes.
2. "Stop."
3. "Start reading one page every two seconds."
   Wait for your alarm clock to ring after three minutes.
4. "Stop."

SPEED MASTERY TECHNIQUE ONE

The different skills practiced in each of the previous exercises are integrated in Speed Mastery Technique One. Many super-reading graduates report that performing this exercise during the workshop permanently increased their reading speed, even if they did not continue practicing this exercise at home as suggested. To get your best reading speed, I recommend that you find the time to practice this exercise four times daily for a period c one month.

How Does This Exercise Work?

This exercise tricks your brain into believing that tex read at higher speeds is actually being read at a slowe speed. Timing yourself with an alarm clock, you read fo four one-minute periods. In the first minute, you read a your best comprehension rate. During the second minute you must double the number of pages you completed ir the first minute. Comprehension is not important now The third minute requires you to triple the amount o pages you read during the first minute. Again, compre hension is not important. Finally, in the fourth minute you once again read at your best comprehension rate— only something wonderful has happened. You're reading faster with excellent comprehension.

Why Does This Exercise Work?

Imagine you want to go jogging on a large track, and it takes you one minute to complete the first lap. Since you have warmed up, you complete your next lap in 45 seconds, and your third lap in only 30 seconds. Feeling a bit tired, you slow down and finish your fourth lap in 50 seconds. But wait, have you really slowed down? Sure, you are running 20 seconds slower than your third min- ute's speed, but 10 seconds quicker than your first minute. Although your running speed appears slower, you actually increased your average speed. Exactly the same situation occurs during reading.

Imagine reading 100 words during the first minute. During the second minute, you scan 200 words per minute, and during the third minute, 300 words per minute. When reading during the fourth minute at 110 words per minute, it feels slow, since it is 190 words slower than the 300 words per minute you tried to read during the third minute. Yet, it is actually 10 percent faster than your first minute's speed. Now you begin the exercise again, reading at 110 words per minute. Doubling and tripling your speed gives you 220 and 330 words per minute. During the fourth minute, you comprehend at 120 words per minute with little trouble. Each time you repeat this exercise your speed will go up until you reach a plateau.

Why Don't You Reach Your Maximum Speed Immediately?

You are learning new reading habits that initially take time for you to perform instinctively. For the first time in many years you will be conscious of reading. Part of your mind needs to focus upon the act of reading as it did when you were a child. Soon, you will be reading instinctively again, able to give your full attention to text, without thinking about reading. When this occurs you will develop an even higher speed. Your full brain power focuses upon reading and not upon thinking about your reading technique.

Speed Mastery Exercise One

Speed Mastery Exercise One will help you read with excellent comprehension at high speed. It consists of four

four-minute exercises that you should perform during single study session. You must not take breaks in th middle of a four-minute session. Perform this exercis four times in a row for a total of 16 minutes for the bes results. I highly recommend that you create a timing tap using the script that follows this exercise.

During this exercise, continually read forward in the text. Immediately following this exercise are a set o important tips. Please read them before attempting t perform the exercise.

(Go to Sample Unit Three, page 224)

1. Read for one minute at your best comprehension rate.
2. During the second minute, continue reading new material. Use a rate that is double your first minute's speed. Do not concern yourself with comprehension during this minute.
3. During the third minute, continue reading new material. Use a rate that is triple your first minute's speed. Do not concern yourself with comprehension during this minute.
4. During the fourth minute, continue reading new material at your best comprehension rate.
5. Repeat this entire exercise three more times.

SCRIPT FOR TAPE

Record the words on each numbered line onto a blank tape. Follow the instructions given in italics, but do not record them onto your tape. To time the exercise, set an alarm clock so that it rings after one minute.

1. "Start reading at your comprehension rate for one minute."
   Wait for your alarm clock to ring after one minute.
2. "Start reading at double your reading rate for one minute."
   Wait for your alarm clock to ring after one minute.
3. "Start reading at triple your reading rate for one minute."
   Wait for your alarm clock to ring after one minute.
4. "Start reading at your best comprehension rate for one minute."
   This exercise should be repeated four times. Record steps 1 through 4 three more times on your tape before beginning the exercise.

Important Tips

1. After completing the first minute of the exercise, quickly mark off the pages in your text that you need to reach at the end of the second and third minutes.
2. During the second minute, do not worry about comprehension; instead, focus solely upon completing your goal on time.
3. During the second minute, you must complete as many pages in the first 30 seconds as you completed during the first minute. During the second 30 seconds, you should again complete as many pages as you read in the first minute. For example, if you read one page during the first minute, you should read two pages during the second minute. If you read 1.5 pages during the first minute, then you should read three

pages during the second minute. Make certain you keep pace with the timing tape.

4. During the third minute, you must complete as many pages in each 20-second interval as you completed during the first minute. For example, if you read one page during the first minute, you should read three pages during the third minute. If you read 1.5 pages during the first minute, then you should read 4.5 pages during the third minute. Make certain you keep pace with the timing tape.

5. Many individuals who have difficulty reading backward find they can use backward reading to increase their speed during minutes two and three of this exercise. Since comprehension is not important during these minutes, it is a wonderful opportunity to master backward reading skills. Many individuals claim that practicing backward reading during these minutes eventually leads to successfully reading backward with comprehension.

6. For peak results, deliberately increase your top speed by a quarter of a page every few days. If you find yourself not comprehending anything, then return to your previous rate. Most likely, you will find that you can read much faster with comprehension than you believed. Usually, it is the fear of missing information that slows you down, rather than your ability to comprehend at higher speed. This exercise will help you conquer that fear so you can achieve your maximum reading speed.

SPEED MASTERY TECHNIQUE TWO

You probably found it impossible to comprehend text during the second and third minutes of the previous exercise. It is possible to comprehend text during these minutes by using topic sentences. The topic sentence found in each paragraph explains its purpose. In non-fiction, the topic sentence usually occupies the top two lines of a paragraph.

During the second and third minutes of this exercise, do not give equal time to all the lines in every paragraph. Instead, slow down to read the topic sentence at your comprehension rate. Make up the time lost from reading the topic sentence by reading more rapidly throughout the rest of the paragraph. Watch for the verbs and nouns that fill in the details of the topic sentence. Your average speed will remain the same, but your rate will vary in critical areas of text containing essential information and will result in comprehension of text at very high speeds. Your ability to comprehend at the highest speeds will vary in accordance with your aptitude in a particular subject.

Speed Mastery Exercise Two

(Go to Sample Unit Three, page 224)

1. Read at your comprehension rate for one minute.
2. Read for one minute at double your reading rate. Slow down to comprehend the topic sentences. Maintain your average reading rate by increasing your speed in the rest of the paragraphs.
3. Read for one minute at triple your reading rate. Slow

down to read the topic sentences. Maintain your average reading rate by increasing your speed in the rest of the paragraphs.

4. Remember to maintain your average reading rate during the second and third minutes. You have not changed the total reading time; instead, you have changed the places where your eye focused in the text. As a result, you obtain the maximum information in the shortest possible time.

In the next chapter I will describe some of the common obstacles to high-speed reading, and how to overcome them.

The Types of Books in Which to Practice Your Speed Mastery Exercises

It is important to select appropriate books to practice your speed mastery exercises. Be certain to use a book that does not challenge your comprehension. Any book that you have difficulty understanding while reading at a slow speed would be inappropriate for these exercises. During an exercise, your only challenge should be reading speed. There are several types of books to choose for your practice sessions.

1. Choose a book on a subject familiar to you. Your schema in this subject should be outstanding and help you comprehend at high speed. For example, a biologist can choose a biology book, an artist an art book.

2. High school history or biology books make excellent choices for practice. The information contained in these texts is familiar to you. It is highly unlikely that

you would read a book on American history and be shocked to learn that we fought the Revolutionary War with Great Britain—and we won!

3. Use a book that you have read and understood several years ago. Your brain will still be familiar with the material.

4. As a rule, nonfiction books are easier to use in your practice than fiction books. Nonfiction books are highly organized and predictable. Fiction books do not have to conform to any specific rules or pattern. For example, a history book will always proceed from an early time period to a later one without skipping back and forth between time periods. On the other hand, a novel can move from the present to the past and then into the future.

Summary

1. You learned how to pace your eye movements by using motion of your hand.

2. Mechanical skills for increasing your reading speed are now familiar to you.

3. You can use topic sentences to obtain comprehension at the highest reading speed.

4. Make certain you initially practice your speed-mastery exercises in books that are not difficult for you to understand at slow reading speeds.

CHAPTER THREE

Schematic Speed-Increasing Techniques

GOALS

- LEARNING HOW TO USE SCHEMA TO INCREASE READING SPEED
- LEARNING HOW TO READ FAMILIAR MATERIAL TO INCREASE READING SPEED
- UNDERSTANDING HOW AUTHORS PROVIDE SCHEMA
- USING VERBS AND NOUNS TO INCREASE READING SPEED
- USING A BOOK'S STRUCTURE TO INCREASE READING SPEED
- RECOGNIZING THE DANGERS OF NEGATIVE AND CONDITIONAL SENTENCES
- USING THE / HAND MOTION
- SOLVING COMMON READING PROBLEMS

HOW TO USE SCHEMA TO INCREASE READING SPEED

Chapter One demonstrated how a lack of schema creates comprehension problems. In Chapter One, remember the difficulty you had in determining that the second exercise was about doing the laundry? Fortunately, in most texts, the opposite situation occurs. Usually, an author provides excessive schema. This extra schema enables you to dramatically increase your reading speed even without the use of the mechanical techniques.

Authors write for an audience, not for a specific individual. They make certain that even the least-prepared reader will obtain the information necessary for understanding the text. When reading, you bring along your unique background and may not require some of the detail, or schema, the author has provided. This is especially true when you read books on familiar subjects. If you understand a subject, your background makes it likely you will find information you already know. An author has no way of determining what you already know or what you need to learn. It is the author's responsibility to provide all the necessary background information required for understanding the book, but it is your responsibility to vary your reading rate as your familiarity with material changes.

HOW TO READ FAMILIAR MATERIAL TO INCREASE READING SPEED

What do most people do when reading about a familiar topic in a difficult book? They slow down. Why? After plodding through a text, finding something familiar is like finding an oasis in a desert. After intense mental work, these easy passages offer a mental resting place. It is human nature to want to rest. Unfortunately, it is a bad reading strategy, and one you should no longer use.

If a book contains new and difficult material, use your time to understand the details. Stop wasting time reading facts you already know. From now on, when you find familiar information, you will be able to increase your reading speed to double or triple your normal rate. You will scan the topic sentences until encountering new information that you require. Then, to facilitate learning this material, you will slow down to your comprehension rate. Make this technique an integral part of your reading habits. Even when reading without using your hands, you can use this reading strategy to force your eyes to scan more rapidly through text.

To illustrate how to use this technique during reading, let's think back to information described in Appendix Two about Pavlov's dog. Classical conditioning is a fundamental concept of modern psychology. Consequently, an author must provide information about classical conditioning when writing any introductory psychology book. An author cannot assume you obtained this information somewhere else. The experiment most often used to illustrate classical conditioning is the story about Pavlov's dog contained in Appendix Two of this book.

When reading your first psychology text, the author's assumption that you do not possess any information about classical conditioning will be correct. While reading about Pavlov's dog, you obtain the schema necessary for understanding other technical psychological concepts.

However, when you read a second psychology book, you already know about this experiment. As soon as you begin to read about the dog drooling over a piece of meat, you will increase your reading speed. You will maintain this higher speed until spotting new material. Using topic sentences, verbs, and nouns, you can determine when to slow down your reading speed to learn new material.

Instead of reading the words on the page, you are reading the concepts formed by the words. You are using schema to comprehend the meaning of text, rather than decoding individual words. This results in excellent comprehension while reading quickly. In the exercise that follows, you will have an opportunity to practice this technique.

Exercise

1. Choose a nonfiction book on a familiar subject.
2. Using your hand motions, begin reading the book at your highest comprehension rate.
3. When you encounter familiar information, increase your reading speed to double or triple your reading rate.
4. Slow down to read the topic sentences, verbs, and nouns that provide the schema of the material.
5. When you encounter new information, once again slow down your reading speed to your highest comprehension rate.
6. Continue practicing this technique in three chapters of your book.
7. For peak performance, continue using this exercise in a different book each day.

HOW AUTHORS PROVIDE SCHEMA

If you analyz a nonfiction book, you will find that concepts and definitions are the two key elements contained in the text. Concepts are the ideas or principles that the author teaches you. Definitions can include names, dates, prices, and any specific information you need to remember.

When presenting a concept, most authors provide an example, anecdote, or illustration to clarify their point. This is part of the schema an author provides to readers. When you find a concept difficult, use this information for additional insight. However, if you do not need the information, then read this data at your fastest speed. Slow down when you encounter new, necessary information.

A good example can be found by considering a typical concept in a self-help book. Imagine reading a book about achieving success in which the author explains that positive thinking helps you attain success. Is this concept confusing to you? Probably not. Yet, if you were really reading about this concept in a self-help book, the author would tell a story to illustrate the point. Imagine the author creates a character named Joe who does not think positively. About ten pages of text discusses Joe's negative thoughts and how they caused him to lose his job, and nearly destroyed his home life. Then Joe read the author's suggestions and began thinking positively. Immediately Joe's life changed for the better. His company rehired him to a more prestigious position, and his family started loving him.

You will no longer plod through sections of text laden with information like this. Instead, by using schema you will be a super reader consciously using the perfect reading speed.

There is another reason that authors provide excessive information. Most authors use an outline consisting of only a few pages. No one would pay for a seven-page outline. By providing examples, illustrations, and anecdotes, the seven-page outline becomes a text of several hundred pages. As a reader, you usually require only the information contained in the original seven-page outline. You must strip the clutter from the text to find the information kernels scattered throughout it. This is primarily true for nonfiction text. In fiction, individual words are often important, so a different reading strategy is necessary and will be described later in this book.

In the following exercise, you will convert an essay back into its key elements. It is constructed so you can see how the mind of a speed reader views text. I placed the concepts and definitions in boldface type so your eyes can easily spot them. Read carefully to see the flow of information contained within the essay. I placed the examples, anecdotes, and illustrations in italic type. When you spot them you should increase your reading speed to double or triple your reading rate. Notice how speeding through this section of text does not diminish your understanding. Instead, it saves you valuable time.

Exercise

1. Read the following essay about the Revolutionary War at your best comprehension rate.
2. Definitions and concepts are placed in boldface type.

3. Examples, anecdotes, and illustrations are placed in italic type.
4. Write down the key elements of the essay, and compare them to the original outline found in Chapter Four, page 73.

America's war for **independence started** near **Boston** that at the time was **occupied by General Gage** of the **British** Army. **War broke out** on the morning of **April 19, 1775** when **700 British regulars** were sent out on a **secret mission** to **destroy** the **American military supplies** in **Concord.**

Paul Revere and William Dawes alerted the American **militia.** *Most of us have heard about Paul Revere and his famous midnight ride. A ride that has been immortalized in poetry and in American literature. Even a few movies have been made about the epic ride taken by the famous silversmith.*

Despite being forewarned, the **American troops** initially were **dispersed** by the **British troops.** American troops stood behind trees, firing shots at the well-trained English soldiers. Soon the **tide of battle turned.** As the **English troops** began **returning to Boston,** many **American militia** began **firing** upon them **from the woods.** *The New England forest made an excellent cover for the troops, preventing the English soldiers from being able to mount a successful attack.* Only **100 American soldiers** were **killed** compared to the **250 British casualties.** *The British would have suffered even greater casualties, but a brigade of their troops was dispatched from Boston to prevent them from being annihilated.*

Word of the **English attack** was **spread by horsemen** who journeyed throughout the Colonies. *Horses were the primary source of transportation in this period. Back in Massachusetts, the* **Massachusetts Committee of Public Safety called for an army of 30,000 to be established to protect the people from British soldiers.** *In response to the call,* **militia came to Boston from all over New England.** This was to set the scene for one of the most famous early battles of the war, the Battle of Bunker Hill, which actually took place on Breed's Hill.

On **June 17th,** *the* **English found the American troops** *occupying* **Breed's Hill.** This hill is on a peninsula overlooking Boston Harbor from the North. *The* **English attacked twice,** *and were* **repulsed by the Americans.** *Finally, the* **Americans ran out of ammunition** and had to **retreat.** *This battle was a great* **moral victory** *for the* **Colonies.** Our soldiers had stood up to the best Britain had to offer. *The* **colonial soldiers** *demonstrated their* **ability to defend themselves** *against Britain's professional army.*

Bunker Hill is best known for the saying, "Don't fire till you see the whites of their eyes." The **muskets** used by the militia were only capable of **accurately** sending a **bullet 50 feet.** To use their weapons effectively, the American troops had to hold their fire until the English soldiers were practically on top of them. This strategy worked. The **British suffered a 40 percent casualty** rate in their assault on the hill.

May 1775 saw another **major American victory.** At this time, the **Green Mountain Boys from Vermont defeated** the **English army guarding Ticonderoga and**

Crown Point. This victory resulted in the **American Army gaining possession of much-needed artillery.**

The **Green Mountain Boys** were under the command of **Ethan Allen.** *Allen was a man known for his outgoing manners and expensive taste in clothes.* At this time, **Vermont was claimed by both New Hampshire and New York. Vermont** colonists **rejected rule by either state,** wanting to **rule themselves** instead. Vermont was determined to become a separate nation, rather than become a part of New York State. Their determination paid off. In **1790** a convention at Bennington ratified the U.S. Constitution, making **Vermont the 14th state on February 18, 1791.**

The day that Fort Ticonderoga fell was also the meeting date for the **Second Continental Congress.** This Congress **sent additional protests to England,** and **requested war supplies and troops from the Colonies. Agents were sent** to **France** to obtain much-needed **financial assistance.** *At this time, the French were bitter enemies of the English. They saw an opportunity to force England into an expensive war in the New World. A war that would weaken the English military presence in Europe. Our revolution presented a political opportunity to France.*

The Second Continental Congress named **George Washington as the Commander In Chief of the Continental Army.** Washington was a wise choice. **Choosing Washington demonstrated** that **England** was **fighting a war** with **all the American Colonies,** and not just at war with New England.

USING VERBS AND NOUNS TO INCREASE READING SPEED

I mentioned how verbs and nouns can help increase your reading speed while maintaining good comprehension. To achieve good comprehension you should be able to answer five key questions. These key questions are *who*, *what*, *where*, *when*, and *why*. Verbs and nouns provide answers to questions. The previous essay about the American Revolution shows how much information the verbs and nouns impart during high-speed reading. Take a look at the nouns and verbs in boldface type in the first sentence of this essay.

America's war for **independence started** near **Boston** which was **occupied by General Gage** of the **British Army.**

America's war . . . independence started . . . Boston . . . occupied by General Gage . . . British Army.

Notice how the verbs and nouns in this sentence hold the essence of its meaning. When reading at high speed, your brain pieces together these fragments into a meaningful whole. Many modern reading examinations make use of this clustering principle by using a technique called *cloze*. In a cloze reading-comprehension test, every few words in the test are deliberately omitted. From a selection of words, you must choose the phrase that best completes the sentence. Your decision is based upon the text surrounding the missing word. The following example will give you an opportunity to answer several questions using the cloze reading technique. This example also illustrates how your brain finds meaning when reading at high speed.

Example

DIRECTIONS: CHOOSE THE WORD THAT YOU BELIEVE BELONGS IN THE BLANK SPACE IN EACH OF THE FOLLOWING SENTENCES.

1. The huge _____ made a loud noise as it flew overhead. (grass, jet)
2. The basketball star threw the _____ through the hoop to win the game. (ball, flower)
3. The _____ sank into the ocean without a trace. (boat, song)
4. Use a _____ to wipe your face while eating. (napkin, shoe)
5. Charles _____ around the track in his new shoes. (ran, radio)

See how easily your mind locates the missing word in each sentence? When reading verbs and nouns at high speeds, your brain easily determines most of the missing text with just as little difficulty. You can read at high speed with good comprehension more efficiently in subjects familiar to you because your schema is higher in these areas.

Scientists claim that the human eye cannot see text at the 25,000-words-per-minute speed at which I read. They are correct. It is not possible to see 25,000 individual words with any comprehension. Instead, I focus upon key elements in a sentence to maintain comprehension. Do you miss important information reading this way? No, because the super-reading program contains many techniques for comprehending text. Learning to use a book's structure is one of these important techniques.

THE SECRETS CONTAINED WITHIN A BOOK'S STRUCTURE

Using a Book's Structure

Usually, the first and last chapter in a book contain a lot of schema. The first chapter introduces the book, discusses its purpose, and what it offers to you. The last chapter usually summarizes the book. It also reviews the information offered in the book, and usually explains additional applications for this information. In some books the last chapter suggests ways for obtaining further information.

These two chapters are very important as Alex, my ten-year-old son discovered while writing book reports in elementary school. Alex is bright, but like a lot of ten-year-olds, can be lazy when doing homework. One Sunday evening he asked for a book that he needed for a report due the next day. It was 9:00 P.M. and I asked him how he expected to finish his work on time.

"No problem. You read the front and back cover. Then the first and last chapter to find out what the book is about, who's in it, and what happens to them. Then you write it down in a report and you get an *A*. The teacher never figures it out."

I felt proud of him for figuring this out, but angry

because he was too lazy to realize that his technique wa
only one of the necessary steps for reading a book fo
school. You do use the information in the first and las
chapters to get the schema of the book, but not for a
complete understanding of its content.

Using the Chapter Structure

Just as the opening and closing chapters hold most of
the schema of a book, the opening and closing paragraphs within each chapter contain the chapter's schema.
The opening paragraph describes the chapter's purpose,
and the closing paragraph summarizes the chapter's
information.

The Dangers of Negative and
Conditional Sentences

During high-speed reading, you may suddenly experience some comprehension difficulty. Some of this difficulty may be due to sentences that are negative or
conditional. Even a single negative or conditional word
can dramatically alter the meaning of a large word
grouping.

Negative sentences are formed by using words that
turn the positive meanings of text into negative ones. For
example, observe how only a single boldface word changes
the meaning of the following sentence.

Positive Sentence: You **can** take some money from my
wallet, and borrow my car for tonight's prom.

Negative Sentence: You **can't** take some money from my wallet, and borrow my car for tonight's prom.

There is quite a difference in meaning between these two sentences. When you start reading at high speed you might miss negative words that alter text, but with practice you can condition yourself to recognize these important words. When spotting a negative word, immediately slow down your reading speed to evaluate its effect upon the surrounding text.

When you begin to spot negative words you are like a new driver learning to spot stop signs. As a new driver, you consciously look for stop signs. Soon, you instinctively know where you are likely to see a stop sign. Your eyes spot the important sign without much effort. Exactly the same thing will happen when you begin consciously searching for negative words. Some common examples of negative words include: *no, not, can't, shouldn't,* and *never.* Make a habit of looking for these words so you can evaluate their impact on surrounding text.

Text containing conditional sentences can affect surrounding text as dramatically as text containing negative sentences. A conditional sentence requires certain conditions to be fulfilled in order for certain things to happen. Words like *if, could,* and *should* are common examples of words found in conditional sentences.

Imagine I told you that I was going to give you a million dollars if. . . . Your immediate response would be to ask, "If what?" Suppose I finished my statement by saying, "If you live to be a million years old." Say good-bye to the million dollars. You already knew that you were not getting the money because the simple two-letter word *if* immediately raised your suspicions. When reading at high speed, be certain that simple conditional words like *if* attract your attention so you can slow down your reading speed long enough to evaluate the implications created by the word.

THE *I* HAND MOTION

As a result of offering hundreds of super-reading workshops, I find the ideal place to introduce an additional hand motion occurs at this point. By now, most students know the fundamental hand motions, and have little difficulty learning the *I* hand motion.

The *I* hand pattern works well in text containing narrow columns. Many students find that a simple back-and-forth motion obscures some of the text in the very narrow columns commonly found in newspapers, magazines, and textbooks. This is not the case with the *I* motion that conforms to the rectangular shape of the columns.

Using the *I* hand motion is simple. You hand moves forward from left to right across the top two lines, and quickly moves down the center of the narrow column, stopping just two lines before the bottom. Then at the bottom two lines, you again move your hand forward from left to right.

Having your eyes read forward at the top and bottom two lines of a column has another important advantage. The top two lines frequently contain the topic sentence which is rich in schematic information. Often, the bottom two lines contain a summary sentence also containing an abundance of schema.

Many people who experience difficulty in reading backward find this the ideal hand motion to use in narrow columns. The forward motion at the top and bottom of a paragraph is identical to the pattern learned in childhood, and the text in narrow columns is easy to see while moving your fingers down the center of text.

Remember, this hand motion is only effective in narrow columns. On a normal page, moving your hand down the center of text will often cause you to miss important word groupings.

EXAMPLE OF THE "I" HAND PATTERN

When should you use the *I* hand motion? Most readers use it to read text efficiently in very narrow columns, like the one you are currently reading. The forward motion at the top two lines helps you comprehend the topic sentence. Reading down the center helps you read the text.

Exercise

1. Obtain a copy of a daily newspaper or magazine.
2. Read for 15 minutes at your comprehension rate, using your *I* hand motion.
3. For advanced work, practice in a different newspaper or magazine each day for one month.

HOW TO SOLVE COMMON READING PROBLEMS

If you were to observe a typical reader's eyes, you might be amazed at how they move across a line of text. Instead of a smooth left-to-right motion, the eyes frequently stop to glimpse words below, above, or to the side of the text. This wasted eye motion reduces reading comprehension while dramatically slowing down reading speed. There are three types of wasted visual movements:

- regressions—looking backward
- progressions—looking forward
- distractions—looking away from the text

All of these visual problems can be prevented by using super-reading skills. Let's begin by examining how to overcome regressions.

Overcoming Visual Regressions

When reading at high speeds, you may experience some difficulty with certain words or phrases that may tempt you to re-read the text to increase your comprehension. When this occurs, remember it is not necessary for you to understand every word or phrase in a text to comprehend its meaning. When encountering a particularly difficult passage, take a pencil and put a small mark in the margin. Later, if you believe you require further study, you can return to your pencil mark.

Our schematic exercise in Chapter One demonstrated

how the meaning of text is contained within its wholeness. Experiencing difficulty within a portion of text is no excuse for slowing down your reading. Continuing to read will often provide the schema you need to obtain comprehension.

Overcoming Visual Progressions

Many readers have a tendency to jump ahead and glance at the words, pictures, or diagrams contained in text. This also reduces reading efficiency and speed without adding any significant comprehension. Super reading makes extensive use of skimming reading materials prior to reading at a comprehension speed. Skimming through a text will acquaint you with its many features. This reduces the likelihood that you will be distracted by a surprising item in the text and prevents visual progressions from slowing down your reading speed.

Overcoming Visual Distractions

Sometimes reading produces mental tension that distracts the mind from focusing upon text. Super reading offers a variety of focusing exercises that enable you to concentrate the full power of your mind upon text. These focusing skills are presented in a later chapter of this book.

Your hand motions also help prevent visual regressions, progressions, and distractions from occurring. These hand motions force your eyes to continue moving forward in the text. The combination of hand motions with the other suggestions just discussed will eliminate all three of these potential reading hindrances.

Vocalization Problems

Many readers find it necessary to say words aloud or silently to themselves while reading. Remember, your brain relies primarily upon your visual sense to comprehend information. Vocalizing words hampers both your efficiency and speed.

Since writing converts spoken language into pictorial form, it is not uncommon to find people lipping words during reading. Some use their lips to pronounce silently each word, while others softly murmur sounds by using their vocal chords or throats. These individuals feel their mind needs to hear the sound of printed text to determine its meaning. This is a fallacy! Schema and other textual clues are all your mind requires to decode text.

Eliminating vocalization can be accomplished in several ways. Some instructors suggest placing a pencil in the mouth to prevent the utterance of sound. Clamping the teeth tightly down on the pencil can be a very effective deterrent to verbalizing words.

The high-speed reading exercises that you use in this course force you to read at a rate far greater than you can speak. During these exercises, you decode text faster than you can speak. For many, this eliminates their vocalization problems.

A complete absence of vocalization is neither required nor desirable. Actually, the opposite is the case. I recommend that every reader verbally abstract and condense the meaning of text when reading at high speed. You do not speak each word aloud. Instead, you summarize the key points and meanings covered in the text as you did with the boldface words in the Revolutionary War essay. This can be done silently, or by speaking softly.

Look back at the second and third exercises in Chapter One. These two exercises drew attention to the importance of schema. Although containing many words, it was challenging to determine that the second exercise was about doing the laundry. The third exercise contained few words, but they were pithy in meaning and easy to comprehend. The many levels of meaning the exercise contained about the relationship between Bob Clarke, Sr. and Bob Clarke, Jr. were easy to see. When reading through text, always try to convert wordy passages into short, schematically rich phrases that you can easily vocalize and retain. This will not only help prevent wasteful vocalization, it also will improve comprehension and retention of text.

There are other reasons why some people read slowly. Many people have a tendency to re-read words. Their eyes scan the text, find a word or phrase that is difficult, and then linger for long periods of time on that passage. They look at it again and again, hoping that soon it might make sense. Usually, all that they obtain is a loss of time. Hand motions help solve this problem by making the eye follow the motion of the hand. If a portion of text appears difficult, your hand keeps moving, pulling your eyes along to new text so that you avoid wasting valuable time on something confusing. You can use your pencil to mark in the margin of the text, indicating the need to come back to this section later and read it at a slower speed. But you don't compromise the time it takes to read the entire text because of this problem in a single section. Often, simply reading further provides the schema necessary for understanding the text.

Summary

1. You can increase your reading speed in familiar material by using the schema to read whole ideas instead of words.

2. Authors provide schema by using examples, illustrations, and anecdotes.

3. Verbs and nouns contain the action and subject in text. They are easily seen while reading at high speed, and useful in summarizing key points in text.

4. The opening and closing chapters in a book contain a great deal of useful schema.

5. The opening and closing paragraphs in a chapter contain a great deal of useful schema.

6. Watch negative or conditional sentences. They can alter the meaning of a large grouping of words.

7. Use the *I* hand motion to read narrow columns.

8. Visual regressions, progressions, and distractions can reduce your reading efficiency. By using hand motions, you can overcome most of the problems caused by them.

CHAPTER FOUR

Tips for Increasing Comprehension

GOALS

- RECOGNIZING THE IMPORTANCE OF JACKET COVERS
- RECOGNIZING THE IMPORTANCE OF COPYRIGHT DATE AND BOOK EDITION
- DISCOVERING THE HIDDEN INFORMATION IN THE FOREWORD
- USING THE INTRODUCTION
- USING THE TABLE OF CONTENTS: A BOOK'S ROAD MAP
- TESTING YOUR COMPREHENSION OF NEW MATERIAL
- MAKING FULL USE OF GRAPHICS
- USING TECHNICAL TABLES AND GRAPHS
- USING SIDEBARS AND FOOTNOTES
- USING SUMMARIES AND ABSTRACTS TO MASTER INFORMATION

- DISCOVERING THE HIDDEN VALUE OF THE INDEX
- USING THE GLOSSARY: AN INVALUABLE STUDY TOOL

THERE'S MORE TO A BOOK THAN ITS COVER

The brain works more efficiently at high speed if a structured search for information is conducted. The better your grasp of a book's schema, the faster you can master high-speed reading. An excellent way to understand a text's schema is by using its layout. This chapter is packed with suggestions for using a book's layout to master quickly all the available schematic information.

KEY QUESTIONS TO ASK

Studying a book's layout to obtain schema is most efficiently accomplished if you look for answers to the following critical questions: *who*, *what*, *where*, *when*, *why*, and *how*. It will help if you imagine a sheet of paper containing blank lines next to each of these questions, somewhat like the following template.

WHO: _____

_____

WHAT: _____

_____

WHERE: _____

_____

WHEN: _____
_____

WHY: _____
_____

HOW: _____
_____

As you examine the different schematically rich sections of a book, find the answers to these important questions. Visualize this information being written on the appropriate lines using short, schematically rich phrases.

THE IMPORTANCE OF JACKET COVER

There may be more to a book than its cover, but the jacket cover is the first place to begin searching for schema. In a bookshop, a book's spine is usually the only visible part of the jacket cover. The title placed on the spine is designed to grab your attention and motivate you to remove the book and read its front and rear jacket covers. Publishers know they must make a sale within seconds, so they design the jacket cover information to convince you to purchase the book immediately. There is a variety of useful information that can be found on jacket covers.

SUMMARIES

Many book jacket covers display a summary of the book's key information. Publishers know that potential readers will not purchase a book if they find the jacket cover difficult to understand, so they create jacket covers that are easy to read. Most jacket covers contain ample blank space to make them easier to read. Since the wording is sparse, all the text contained on a jacket cover is densely packed with schema.

Reading a summary will enable you to determine the book's purpose. Match your purpose to the book's to determine if the material is worth investing your time. This is particularly true when you have limited time and several potential books to read.

Biographies

Biographical information describes the author's qualifications and experience. This information can help you evaluate the author's expertise on a subject. You must determine if anything in the author's background affects the author's ability to write objectively.

Reviewers' Comments

Many publishers print favorable comments by recognized reviewers on a jacket cover. The value of this information depends upon your familiarity with the reviewer's work. A publisher is not going to show you any unfavorable reviews the work has received. Even a poorly written text will receive some favorable comments that can be included on a jacket cover to entice an unwary reader. Sometimes a professional relationship or friendship exists between the reviewer and either the publisher or author. This relationship may bias the value of the review. Be aware of this when using a review as a source of information about a book.

Endorsements by Authorities

An endorsement by a recognized authority is usually more reliable than a review. Individuals respected in a field will seldom compromise their reputations by saying things they do not believe. This is true unless the endorser stands to gain financially by recommending the book. If you suspect an endorsement does financially benefit an expert, then accept the accuracy of their statements with much skepticism. Endorsements by authorities with impeccable reputations can add significant validity to a text.

Picture of the Author

Many fictional works contain a picture of the author on the front or back jacket covers. Your familiarity with the writing style and reputation of the author is what helps the publisher market the text. Unless the author is a recognizable authority whose picture helps you identify the value of the work, you are less likely to find the picture of an author on the cover of a nonfiction book. The author's picture usually provides little schematic information about the text.

Jacket Flaps

The typical jacket flap contains a summary or review of a book. I recently had the opportunity to witness the importance of a book jacket flap. I was a guest on *After Drive*, a show on the *HA Comedy Network*. The producer wanted me to read Jackie Collins's book, *Lady Boss*, in less than five minutes, and did not want me reading the book before the taping. During rehearsal they required shots of my hands rubbing the book in order to properly position the cameras, so they let me read the jacket flap of the book to get the perfect camera angle. It is lucky that I read the jacket flap because it contained biographies of the main characters. Many characters' first names started with the letter *M*. This similarity made identifying characters at high speed very difficult. Fortunately, the time I spent reading their biographies on the jacket flap enabled me to accurately recognize their names in an instant. Reading the jacket flap enabled me to comprehend the book in five minutes, otherwise the interview would have been a disaster. Instead, I was invited to appear on four more episodes of the show, making me their most frequently invited guest. I owed a considerable debt to that jacket flap. You may not have to read a book in five minutes on national television, but you will find the jacket cover and flaps an invaluable source of quick information about a book.

COPYRIGHT DATE AND BOOK EDITION

It only takes a second to check the copyright date and book edition, but it can make a significant difference in the value of the material. After being submitted to a publisher, it takes almost a year for a book to be published. As a result, even the most up-to-date book is usually at least one year behind in accuracy. In some subjects, books are outdated even before they are published.

A wise reader makes certain the information in a book is as current as possible. You should contrast recent information published in newsletters and magazines with data contained in the book before formulating opinions based upon the information the book contains.

Sometimes having an out-of-date book can be an advantage. It offers the perspective of someone living in the past, before other information became available. When writing something requiring a historical perspective, this type of literature can prove invaluable. Knowing the copyright date is essential when you use this information.

THE HIDDEN INFORMATION IN THE FOREWORD

The foreword of a book is the only place in the text where either another author or a recognized authority talks about the author. Students should *always read* the foreword to a book, but rarely do. Many have the attitude that it is bad enough to have to read assignments in a book, so why would they want to read a portion of the book that is not assigned? The answer is simple. Inferential reading begins with a study of the foreword. In the foreword you learn about the background, experience, training, and qualifications of the author. Information that is essential for determining the reliability of the author.

Imagine a new book titled *Israel*. How different would your opinion of the book be if the author's name was either Moishe Dyan or Yassar Arafat? Do you honestly think that the book would be written by both men in the same way? Of course not! Your schema alerts you to the significant relationship both these men have with Israel. A relationship that most definitely would affect the validity and reliability of both books. Not every author is as well-known as these two men. It is the foreword that reveals the details of an author's life. It is vital for readers to understand the influences that have shaped the author's opinions.

As a reader, you need to know where an author grew up. This reveals the kind of environment and culture that shaped their beliefs and attitudes. If an author harbors unusual opinions, you must consider how these influences affected the author's opinion before using the information.

Always consider the experience and training that qualify the author as an expert. While college training may not always be a necessary credential, in certain academic subjects it does add considerable respectability to the author's opinion if the author was educated at a distinguished institution.

Observe which individuals the author acknowledges as important influences. Do you recognize these individuals as respected experts on the subject or are they considered eccentric by many of their colleagues? Make certain that individuals having opinions differing from the author's and mentioned in the foreword are also discussed in the text. If an author omits mentioning responsible individuals having different opinions, it is possible that the text is slanted, biased, and opinionated.

History is filled with examples of nations becoming

subverted by writers who effectively presented biased opinions. Consider Hitler's book *Mein Kampf*. Hitler presented his perverted philosophy in a form that appealed to the desperate people of Germany. This resulted in the most civilized nation in the world at that time turning into a barbaric horde, slaying and mutilating other human beings. Fortunately, most books do not have the same drastic effect upon civilization, but many still create crippling harm to innocent people when readers fail to evaluate carefully the truthfulness of the information they contain.

Typically, a foreword is written by someone who either knows the author or is another expert on the subject matter. These individuals often reveal facts that can completely alter your opinion of a book—even one you previously read and thought you understood. An excellent example of this can be found in political science.

Karl Marx, famous for his work, *Das Kapital*, had a chronic case of boils that were so painful that he could not sit his entire adult life. Many political scientists and philosophers ponder what the world might have been like if Marx had been healthy. His work reflected the thoughts of a person in terrible pain, and this affliction definitely affected his perspective of life.

This information is found in a foreword, and is information that might not be found anywhere else in a book. If you previously read Marx's famous work, did this new information alter some of your thoughts on it? Of course it did. Remember this example and develop a habit of reading the foreword of a book. If you want to read inferentially, the foreword is not optional reading.

HOW TO USE THE INTRODUCTION

A book's purpose is described in its introduction. When you have several books to consider using for a project, you should scan their introductions to determine which ones best fulfill your purpose.

In an introduction, an author describes why the book was written. Use this information to determine the author's motive and objectives. If the author tries to influence your opinion on a subject, this information is crucial in determining how much you can trust the author.

Exercise

1. Choose a nonfiction book on a subject of interest to you.
2. Analyze the date of the publication to determine the reliability of the information.
3. Analyze the information contained on the jacket cover, jacket flaps, foreword, and introduction to answer the questions contained in the following outline.
4. Go to a library and choose books having different types of information on their jacket covers, and repeat steps 1 and 2.
5. Create additional templates on a blank sheet of paper.

OUTLINE FOR USE WITH EXERCISE

RELIABILITY: _____
_____

WHO: _____
_____

WHAT: _____

_____

WHERE: _____

_____

WHEN: _____

_____

WHY: _____

_____

HOW: _____

_____

INFLUENCES: _____

_____

HOW TO USE THE TABLE OF CONTENTS: A BOOK'S ROAD MAP

Whenever I take a long trip in my car, I first go to the automobile club to obtain a *triptik*. A *triptik* is a map of the journey describing everything I will encounter along my route. Even before I leave my home, I know where every restaurant, motel, and place of interest will be located. The table of contents is a reader's road map of the book. It describes where the author will take you, and how the author plans to get you there. To retain this important information you should always read the table of contents at your comprehension speed.

The table of contents usually contains the information an author provided the publisher in order to sell the book. Contrary to popular belief, authors often sell their books before rather than after writing them. Publishers do not have the time and resources to read complete manuscripts on every idea presented to them. Instead, they use the table of contents and other information to evaluate the marketability of a book. Since the table of contents is the author's outline, it is an important feature that everyone should read.

Patterns Used for Contents

Every book's table of contents is based upon a pattern. Examine your book's table of contents to determine what type of pattern the author employed. Books within a specific subject use patterns distinctive to the subject area. For example, a history book always flows from the past into the present. It never begins in the present, jumps to prehistoric times, and then jumps into World War I. No school would purchase a history book that treated time so erratically. Consequently, history books follow a temporal formula moving from the past into the present. The following sample portion of a table of contents from a typical American history book provides an example of this temporal flow.

AMERICAN HISTORY

PART ONE
FREEDOM IN THE NEW WORLD

CHAPTER FIVE
THE NEW NATION

PART TWO
STARTING THE AMERICAN REPUBLIC

CHAPTER SIX
THE CONSTITUTION OF THE
UNITED STATES

In a biology book, the typical table of contents pattern arranges things from smaller to larger units of size. For example, the unit on the cell would precede the unit on tissue. By examining the table of contents in a biology book, you see parallels in its structure that are carried forward throughout the text. Notice how each organism in Unit Three, Vertebrate Biology, follows a pattern moving in the order of physiology, mating, and eating. Most science texts follow this predictable and structured style in their contents. Below is a sample portion of a table of contents from a biology book.

HUMAN BIOLOGY ONE

UNIT ONE

THE STRUCTURE OF LIVING THINGS
PART ONE

PART TWO
THE STAGES OF LIFE

CHAPTER THREE
CELLS AND ORGANISMS

CHAPTER 4
SPECIES

CHAPTER 5
POPULATIONS

CHAPTER 6
ECOSYSTEMS

CHAPTER 7
THE BIOSPHERE

UNIT TWO

LIFE OPERATIONS
PART THREE

METABOLISM IN LIVING SYSTEMS
CHAPTER EIGHT
NUTRITION

CHAPTER NINE
RESPIRATION IN LIVING SYSTEMS

UNIT THREE

VERTEBRATE BIOLOGY
PART FOUR
COMPARISON OF VARIOUS VERTEBRATES

CHAPTER 11
FISH

CHAPTER 12
AMPHIBIANS

CHAPTER 13
REPTILES

You can use a book's table of contents to obtain a perspective of its structure. During reading, if a portion of text is puzzling or difficult, you can use the pattern found in the table of contents to find other sections in the text that provide information that will help you comprehend the difficult portion. For example, if you notice that an appendix at the end of a mathematics book contains sample problems, you may want to refer to it when having difficulty with a new math concept. This practice may be all you need to comprehend the new math principle. By using the table of contents in this fashion, you can overcome many of the comprehension difficulties you encounter.

Exercise

1. Use the sample table of contents from a history book to answer the questions and fill in the schematic information on the blank lines.

2. Repeat this exercise using the sample table of contents from the biology book.

HISTORY BOOK SCHEMA

WHO: _____

_____

WHAT: _____

_____

WHERE: _____

_____

WHEN: _____

_____

WHY: _____

_____

HOW: _____

_____

PATTERN: _____

BIOLOGY BOOK SCHEMA

WHO: _____

_____

WHAT: _____
_____

WHERE: _____
_____

WHEN: _____
_____

WHY: _____
_____

HOW: _____
_____

PATTERN: _____
_____

HOW TO TEST YOUR COMPREHENSION OF NEW MATERIAL

Most people read a text without questioning or challenging the author's information. This is passive reading. A super reader is an active reader, someone who questions and challenges everything in a text. During reading you should formulate the three types of questions regarding textual meaning described at the beginning of this book: *literal*, *implied*, and *inferential*.

Asking literal questions tests your recall of the specifics mentioned in text. Asking implied questions tests your understanding of the suggestions made by the text. Asking inferential questions reveals if you possess an understanding of the text's deeper significance. If you have a problem formulating any of these questions, it indicates that you do not have a mastery of the text. It is better to discover this on your own by asking questions, rather than at a meeting or while taking an examination. This is not only potentially embarrassing, but you also may suffer consequences of greater significance.

Asking questions during reading helps you remember the information. It forces your mind to focus intensely upon facts and information. Mentally focusing upon information helps you to permanently retain the information. Questioning forces your mind to analyze information until it makes sense, increasing the likelihood that you will remember the information later. Research on memory indicates that you do not remember things unless you understand them.

An excellent book in which to practice answering questions is a high school history book. Go to a library to obtain one that you can use during your high-speed reading practice. After answering the questions asked in the text, create several new questions of your own. Once you get accustomed to asking the types of questions found in the history book, you will have no difficulty doing it on your own with a more challenging book.

Exercise

1. Create a specific question on the information contained in this chapter, and then answer it.
2. Create an implied question on the information contained in this chapter, and then answer it.
3. Create an inferential question on the information contained in this chapter, and then answer it.

SAMPLE QUESTIONS

SPECIFIC QUESTION: What is unique about the information contained in books' forewords?
ANSWER: The forewords of books are the one place in their texts where authors talk freely about themselves.

IMPLIED QUESTIONS: What pattern would you expect to see in a table of contents in a zoology book?
ANSWER: The table of contents would probably contain information about each type of animal and the information about each would follow a similar pattern.

INFERENTIAL QUESTION: How would you read a book lacking a table of contents?

ANSWER: You would read the book at triple reading speed, observing the flow of information it contains. Using this information, you would mentally create a simple table of contents, which you would use to enhance your understanding when reading at a comprehension rate.

HOW TO MAKE FULL USE OF GRAPHICS

Publishers dislike including graphs and diagrams in books because they significantly increase production costs. Yet, publishers frequently include them. Why? Graphics provide essential visual schema that readers need in order to comprehend a book. Imagine trying to master a textbook on the anatomy of the heart without having a diagram of the heart's anatomy. Would you want a doctor performing surgery on your heart whose only experience was a textbook filled with words and devoid of all diagrams? I doubt it.

Remember, vision is the primary sense of human beings. Visual clues enable our brains to work at peak efficiency. Graphs and diagrams summarize complex data so our brains can more easily assimilate it.

One of the finest magazines that uses diagrams is *Scientific American*. Each article starts with a summary that provides the essential schema necessary for understanding the article. Next, a liberal amount of labeled diagrams accompany the text. These labels summarize the key points made in the text. Reading the summary and labeled diagrams gives you about 80 percent of the information contained within each article.

Exercise

1. Purchase a recent issue of *Scientific American*, or obtain one from a library.
2. Read the summary and labeled diagrams for each article.
3. Write down what you believe each article is about.
4. Read each article's total text.
5. Compare the information obtained from step 2 with the information obtained from reading the entire article.
6. Notice how much of the information you can obtain by simply reading the visual information.
7. Choose a magazine you enjoy that uses pictures, and repeat this exercise.

HOW TO USE TECHNICAL TABLES AND GRAPHS

Many texts contain technical tables that make comprehension difficult even when reading slowly. When reading a text containing technical tables, do not attempt to learn the table's information. Instead, see what type of information the table provides. For example, if an accounting test contains a tax table describing payroll deductions for a married individual, you simply remember this topic. You do not memorize all the deductions contained within the table. If you need to know the details, place a small line in the margin next to the table. This indicates that the information contained in the table needs to be memorized after you have completed your reading. Remember that memorizing information is a separate step from reading. Use your top reading speed to locate technical information that you need to master, then use the memory techniques described in this book to retain the information.

Exercise

1. Read the following table at your highest comprehension speed.

SAMPLE TABLE

MONTH	MONTHLY SALES REPORT Number of Monthly Sales	Cash Amount of Sales
JANUARY	50	$5,000

FEBRUARY	80	$8,000
MARCH	40	$4,000
APRIL	10	$1,000
MAY	90	$9,000
JUNE	15	$1,500
JULY	8	$8,000
AUGUST	25	$2,500
SEPTEMBER	75	$7,500
OCTOBER	85	$8,500
NOVEMBER	13	$1,300
DECEMBER	93	$9,300

2. After completing your reading, write down what you recall in the following space:

_____

_____

Most people would not be able to recall the actual figures found in the various columns. What you see at high speed is the title of this table, revealing that it contains information about monthly sales figures. You also might see which months were included, and have a rough idea of the types of sales being made at the company. If you required the specific information in this table, you would use super-reading memory techniques after completing your reading.

If you view a graph while reading at high speed, read the title to determine the nature of the information it contains. Should you need to memorize the information, then mark off the graph with a small check mark in the margin and use the memorization techniques to master its contents after completing your reading of the chapter at high speed.

There are several methods for determining what information needs to be mastered for school or business purposes. These methods are described in detail in a later chapter of this book.

HOW TO USE SIDEBARS AND FOOTNOTES

A sidebar is a small story within a story in a magazine or book that is usually set off by a graphic box or line. Usually, sidebars contain important background information that a reader requires in order to understand the story.

A magazine that uses sidebars well is *Time* magazine. When *Time* ran a story about the student rebellion in China, the story contained many references to key Chinese political figures and officials with whom many *Time* readers would not have been familiar. To solve this problem, *Time* used a sidebar displaying the biographies of each of the important political figures the story mentioned. The sidebar gave readers the schema about each of the important figures described in the story.

Some texts contain footnotes that are similar in function to sidebars. Footnotes also contain background information you may need to comprehend a text.

It is easy to determine if you need to read sidebars or footnotes in a text. Use your highest reading speed to scan the topic sentences in the sidebars or footnotes in order to determine the types of information they contain. If you recognize this information, you can continue reading a text without reading footnotes or sidebars. But if they contain new information, you should read them before completing a text.

A good example of text containing many footnotes is a typical high school book that includes a play by Shakespeare. The footnotes identify the historical information necessary for understanding the play's plot. Sometimes the footnotes define the meaning of an old English word by giving its modern form so that you can comprehend the true meaning of the word.

Exercise

1. Go to a local library and find a play by Shakespeare that contains numerous footnotes.
2. Practice reading a chapter without using the footnotes, then practice reading a chapter using the footnotes.
3. Observe how the schema contained within the footnotes helps you obtain better comprehension of the text.

HOW TO USE SUMMARIES AND ABSTRACTS TO MASTER INFORMATION

Certain texts provide summaries or abstracts of information that they contain. This is a source of information to a reader; especially if the subject matter is unfamiliar. Authors use summaries or abstracts to highlight what they hope you will learn from their writing.

If a text contains either a summary or an abstract, read the information they contain at your best speed. Frequently reflect upon information while reading the text. This information often comes at the end of a chapter.

Summaries are often found in textbooks. Authors place them to help students identify the most important information a chapter contains. If you cannot identify this information after reading the summary, go to the beginning of the chapter and study until you are familiar with it. If an author considers information important enough to list separately in a summary, you should place a heavy emphasis on it. Often, this information plays an important role in a later chapter of the book, so the author is making certain you are aware of its importance by placing it in a chapter summary.

Abstracts are used in technical and legal journals to condense lengthy text into short, meaningful units that can be read quickly. You use abstracts to determine if the information contained in the text is worth investing your time.

THE HIDDEN VALUE OF THE INDEX

Most people think of the index as a feature for finding what page contains specific information. Almost no one would consider it something to read in every book. Actually, reading the index is an important thing you can do to measure your familiarity with the book's content. Unlike the table of contents that should be read at a comprehension rate, you should read the index at triple your reading speed.

In my many lectures, people often complain of misjudging how difficult a book will be to understand. Often the early chapters in a book are easy. Even difficult subjects like calculus and chemistry appear easy in the first few chapters of a book. Individuals erroneously base the difficulty level of the entire book on these early chapters, only to find out that the book is more difficult than they estimated. Unfortunately, by the time they discover how much more time will be required to learn the information, they no longer have any extra time available.

Skimming the index eliminates this problem by making you aware of the total content of a book. While reading, you can determine if the key words appearing in it are familiar or unknown to you. An index with many familiar words indicates the book will not be difficult for you to understand, while one with many unfamiliar terms is a warning that you must be prepared to allocate more time for understanding the book. Remember to spend no more than five minutes reading an index. The bulk of your time should be spent reading the book.

HOW TO USE THE GLOSSARY: AN INVALUABLE STUDY TOOL

If skimming an index is a quick way to determine your familiarity with the content of a book, skimming a glossary reveals your familiarity with the vocabulary of a subject. Just like reading an index, you read the glossary at triple your speed to measure your recognition of words contained within the book. Encountering familiar words indicates the book will be easy for you to understand, while seeing many new words means you should allow yourself extra time to understand the material.

A glossary offers help to students who need to pass examinations. Many of the word-identification questions found in fill-in-the-blank and multiple-choice questions are located in the glossary. Studying the vocabulary words in a glossary helps ensure high grades on examinations that utilize word-identification questions. You will learn additional skills for studying in a later chapter of this book.

Anyone starting to learn a new subject should spend time reading the glossary. Nothing reveals a lack of knowledge more than misusing key words in a subject. If your work requires using specialized terms, reading a glossary is a quick way to find the words you need to learn.

Summary

1. Keep asking *who, what, where, when, why,* and *how* while reading.
2. Jacket covers and flaps provide summaries, biographies, reviewer's comments, endorsements, and other schematically rich information.
3. Always check the copyright date to determine if your material is up-to-date.
4. Authors provide important information about themselves in introductions that can help you evaluate if they have any hidden motives or objectives in their work.

5. The table of contents is the author's book outline. You can use it to see how the book is structured.

6. Practice reading actively by asking literal, implied, and inferential questions about the material in your text. Constantly challenge and corroborate the author's points with other information you possess on the subject.

7. Use tables and graphs to obtain the visual schema the author provides. Remember, at high speed it is not possible to comprehend the details contained in tables and graphs. Simply focus upon the schemata they contain, and determine if you need to memorize their content using the memory techniques offered in this program.

8. Sidebars and footnotes provide additional information that a reader may require to comprehend the material contained in text. Read them at high speed to determine if the information they contain is familiar to you.

9. Summaries and abstracts should always be read before you attempt to comprehend the text. During reading, look for the information they contain in the main body of the text.

10. Skimming an index can save you much grief. If you find that many of the topics are difficult and unfamiliar, then make certain you allow yourself sufficient time to understand the material.

11. A glossary provides a summary of the vocabulary you need to know about a subject. Skim the glossary to determine if you need extra time to learn many new vocabulary words.

CHAPTER FIVE

Reading for Comprehension

GOALS

- MASTERING THE THREE STEPS FOR COMPREHENSION READING
- UNDERSTANDING THE FOUR MOTIVES FOR READING
- MASTERING STRATEGIES FOR DIFFERENT TYPES OF READING
- LEARNING HOW TO DEVELOP A FLEXIBLE APPROACH TO READING

THE THREE STEPS FOR COMPREHENSION READING

There are many different reasons for reading. Each reason requires a different strategy. Reading technical information for an examination requires using skills inappropriate when reading for relaxation. Most reading falls between these two extremes. There are three distinct steps you can use to read with the most efficient blend of speed and comprehension. As you vary the materials you read, you also vary the use of these steps to fit your specific purposes. This chapter is loaded with information on the best reading strategies available for your different reading objectives.

Initially, you may find the sensation of learning information at high speed strange. Especially if you attempt to absorb everything the text contains. This is a wasteful and time-consuming way to read. During super reading, you learn information in stages with an awareness of what options are available to maximize your comprehension. You never waste time learning unnecessary information; instead, you use the time saved to read more while mastering the technical information that you must know.

Overview of the Three Steps

Productive skimming is the first step when reading for comprehension. Reading at two to five seconds per page makes you aware of a text's schema. It is easy to complete an average text in less than ten minutes at this speed. Observe the layout and other distinctive features containing important schema. Rocketing through a text reveals how information is distributed throughout it. Place check marks and asterisks in the left margin to highlight information you need to read carefully at a comprehension rate.

Once you are aware of the text's features, you then enter the second reading stage. Go to the beginning of the text and read at your best comprehension rate. This slower rate permits you to observe the finer points of the text. Again, place check marks and asterisks in the margin to highlight areas of text that you need to memorize. These marks can also be placed next to areas of text you find difficult to comprehend. Instead of slowing down your reading speed, you return to these highlighted sections later and study them at a much slower pace.

During the third reading phase, go to the highlighted areas so you can spend time analyzing these important sections. Often, your consciousness of the text obtained from the schema you have already found helps you decode these difficult portions. This takes far less time than if you had stopped to slowly master each fact when you first saw it. Now is when you should study and memorize any important concepts or definitions.

Highlighting: The Key to Remembering Important Text

While skimming and reading at your best comprehension rate, inspect the text for key points, ideas, and definitions that need to be understood and remembered. Draw a straight line in the left margin to mark off the area of the text containing this important information.

Highlighting text using marks in the margin is less expensive than using a marking pen, and takes less time. Marking text with a highlighter requires you to stop reading, open the cap on the marker, mark off a specific portion of the text, and then close the cap to prevent the felt from drying out. Halting your hand motion to perform these tasks causes a loss of valuable reading time.

A straight line in the margin codes information that you need to spend more time learning. I also use an asterisk (*) to mark off text that I must memorize. It is easy to turn a line into an asterisk by simply drawing the letter x through it. After reading the information highlighted by a straight line, you may decide to upgrade the importance of the line to an asterisk, indicating the information must now be memorized and not simply comprehended. I recommend using only a line or asterisk as highlighting codes. Using more symbols slows down your reading and reduces your productivity.

When reading text requiring highlighting, hold your pencil in your hand. Use your pencil as you would your finger to guide your eyes through the text. This permits you to stop and quickly draw a line or asterisk in the margin without any appreciable decrease in your reading rate. It is a good idea to keep a note pad handy to mark down key points picked up in the text during highlighting.

Step One: Productive Skimming

During productive skimming, your primary goal is to read the text's units of meaning rather than its individual words. Using the text's schema, you can comprehend its meaning at very high speed. No more than two to five seconds should be spent on any particular page during this stage of reading. Spend your time learning about the text, rather than the details the text's information contains. Attentively view the text's features. Does it contain columns, chapters, or any other features you can utilize? Mark off these areas so you can read them later at your comprehension rate.

Often at my seminars, people describe their specific reading problems. A common problem I often hear people talking about is how much time they lose trying to understand a difficult passage in a book. During ordinary reading, the eyes move at a constant pace from the front to the back of a book. This contributes to the difficulty people have in understanding difficult text. As you saw earlier in this book, comprehension problems are often directly linked to a reader's schema. If a reader lacks the schema an author assumes the reader possesses, comprehending a text can often be impossible. Sometimes this missing schema is in the text that appears later in the book rather than the text they are currently reading. Productive skimming helps eliminate this problem.

Complete a book in under ten minutes, using productive skimming to obtain an overview of the book's schematic content. If you later find a difficult passage of text, instead of wasting valuable time trying to comprehend it, turn to the area of the book containing the helpful schematic information.

HOW TO SKIM PRODUCTIVELY

Read each page in two to five seconds during productive skimming. Zipping through the book, your eyes will see the information, but your inner voice will not be able to verbalize the words being read. Remember, it is not necessary to completely silence this inner voice. Use your inner voice to condense or summarize key textual points. Not only will this eliminate the verbalization of individual words, but it will also focus your mind upon the information and help you comprehend it more clearly. Focusing by using your inner voice strengthens both comprehension and retention of the printed information.

Initially, during high-speed reading, it seems as if nothing is being learned. Despite this feeling, your mind absorbs substantial information. After performing the following exercise you will become more aware of the type of information your mind instinctively absorbs during productive skimming.

Exercise

1. Choose a nonfiction book on a familiar topic.
2. Read each page of the book in two to five seconds.
3. Use your hand to move your eye fast enough to complete each page in the required amount of time.
4. Spend no more than ten minutes reading the book. In a lengthy book, read three to five chapters, and scan the book's other important features.

What information did you obtain from your book during this exercise? Although it seems you did not comprehend the material, your mind absorbed considerable information about:

- the book's type size
- the number of columns per page
- information contained on the book's jacket covers and flaps
- the average length of sentences and words in the book
- important features the book contains or lacks

TYPE SIZE

Type size varies not only between different books, but also can vary within the same book. Authors use larger typeface to highlight headings or key information. Footnotes, quotes, and lengthy technical data are often printed using smaller typeface.

Older readers often require brighter lighting when reading books containing small print. Good resolution of small typeface requires bright lighting. If your productive skimming of a text reveals your book contains small print, arrange for a well-lit reading environment that will help reduce eyestrain while enhancing your comprehension.

Large typeface makes words easier to read, and fewer words appear on each page. Authors frequently use larger typeface to highlight schematically important regions of a book, making books that contain large typeface easier to read at high speed.

Combining your awareness of the size of a book's typeface with the other information obtained from the foreword, introduction, index, and glossary helps you make a good estimate of how long a book will take to comprehend.

NUMBER OF COLUMNS CONTAINED IN A TEXT

Columns often appear in newspapers and magazines, but many textbooks also use them. A column format makes it easier to understand information because your eyes have fewer words to scan per line. Highlighted words are also easier to find in columns. Remember to use the *I* hand motion described in Chapter Three to read text printed in columns.

THE IMPORTANCE OF THE NUMBER OF CHAPTERS AND THEIR LENGTHS

To estimate a book's difficulty, you must analyze the number of chapters and their lengths. Knowing that a book contains many lengthy chapters indicates a need to allocate extra reading time to master it.

Most nonfiction books use chapters to organize information into easy-to-learn units. Although a book containing shorter chapters should be easier to comprehend, you must also consider your familiarity with this subject area. Even lengthy chapters are easy to read in a familiar subject, while short chapters may prove difficult if the material is unfamiliar to you.

In many fiction books, chapters are an optional feature. Their presence or absence depends upon the writing style of the author. Since chapters structure a book's information, a lack of chapters make a story more difficult to comprehend at high speed.

SKIMMING JACKET COVERS AND FLAPS

Read both the jacket covers and flaps of a book during your productive skimming. I recommend reading at a five-to-ten-second-per-page rate because book jacket covers and flaps typically contain a great deal of schematically useful information that is worth investing a bit more time in.

COPYRIGHT DATE

During your skimming, take a moment to check the copyright date of your book. Keep this date actively in your mind while evaluating the usefulness of the other information you view during your initial high-speed reading. If the subject is familiar to you, contrast the book's information with data you have obtained in more recent publications. Make certain your book contains information that is current and accurate enough for your purpose. For example, an accountant can not use tax laws from ten years ago to perform a current tax return. Accountants require the most recent tax law information. Although some information retains its value for a certain time period, use your expertise in a subject to determine if the copyright date makes your book an unreliable source.

SKIMMING GRAPHICS

Does your book contain any tables, graphs, or diagrams that you can use for better understanding? Skim to find any graphics your book provides. Do not attempt to master the visual information while skimming the book. This will consume too much time. Your objective is to discover if your book contains useful visual information, and to place a check mark or asterisk in the margin to highlight any important information found.

SKIMMING ACKNOWLEDGEMENTS

Acknowledgements are not featured in every book. Look for them at the beginning or rear of your book. Establish if your book contains this information, and quickly scan the cited names to determine if any are familiar to you.

SKIMMING THE FOREWORD AND INTRODUCTION

Look for a foreword or introduction at the beginning of your book. If your book contains either feature, slow down so that you are reading at ten seconds per page. Use this information to start your inferential reading of the book, as described in Chapter Four.

THE TABLE OF CONTENTS

The important information contained in the table of contents should be read at ten seconds per page. Remember to analyze the structural pattern it contains as well as its general content.

SKIMMING THE BOOK'S MAIN BODY

The size of a book's main body determines how many pages you should read when skimming. If you can complete the book's main body within five to ten minutes, then you should read the entire text. In a long book, you must use a different strategy.

Imagine reading a large textbook. Skimming its every page serves no purpose. Most likely, you would not remember most of the material. The table of contents provides the same schematic information in a more condensed format that is easier for you to remember. If your textbook contains units, then read one or two of them. Often, the end of a unit contains special features like summaries which are not found at the end of each chapter. If the textbook contains chapters without units, then reading three to five chapters will provide sufficient information about the chapters' format.

Always skim the sections at the rear of a book to determine if it contains an index, glossary, or appendices containing important information. Skim the rear of every book, even if you do not skim every chapter in it.

SKIMMING THE INDEX AND GLOSSARY

Take three minutes to skim the index and glossary if your book contains either of these features. Use the techniques described in the last chapter to determine the book's difficulty level based upon these features.

APPENDICES

Scan appendices carefully to identify any important information they may contain. Many books summarize key points in an appendix. For example, computer books list in a special appendix the common problems you might encounter in using a program. If you're using the book to solve a problem, you might want to read this appendix before going to other sections. Many science and math textbooks provide sample problems along with their solutions in an appendix. If you experience difficulty with a section of the book related to this type of problem, you should turn to the appendix to practice solving the problems.

Read the pages in an appendix at two to three seconds per page. Your goal is not to memorize the information, but to become aware of the information contained in your book's appendices.

SKIMMING A BOOK'S SPECIAL FEATURES

Authors vary the appearance of portions of text to call your attention to particular words and phrases. While skimming, see if your book uses any special features that may include:

- larger typeface
- boldface
- italics
- boxes
- lines
- color

Your eyes can easily pick out portions of text that appear different from the rest of a book. Give special attention to these portions of text during your initial skimming. Usually, these portions contain schematically important information.

In the following exercise you will have the opportunity to productively skim a relatively technical essay about the human brain. If you make use of the text's special features, you will be able to comprehend its key points. Note that unless you possess a strong biology background, it is unlikely the technical information in this essay will be meaningful to you at high speed. Reading this passage will duplicate the type of experience you will have when quickly reading technical information. Key points will be seen, the type of information described will be understood, but the specifics will not be easy to comprehend or remember.

Exercise

1. Read the following exercise at your two-seconds-per-page rate.
2. Focus your eyes upon the words in large type, and write down what you remember about the content of the text on the lines below:

_____

_____

_____

_____

_____

_____

_____

_____

_____

_____

_____

_____

_____

_____

_____

_____

THE HUMAN BRAIN

INTRODUCTION

Over 14 billion *neurons*, or nerve cells, link together in this incredible organ. So close together are these cells that it is believed that the action of any single cell has an effect upon several of its neighbor cells.

The brain operates in harmony with the rest of the body. Information concerning the conditions in the various regions of the body reach the brain through links in the nervous system. Chemicals carried in the blood also are analyzed by the brain, and are responsible for many important actions taken by the brain.

STRUCTURE OF THE BRAIN

Seen from the top, the brain appears to be divided into two halves that are partially separated. Beneath these hemispheres are the various structural units of the brain. There are three main subdivisions in an adult human brain: **the hindbrain, midbrain, and forebrain.**

THE HINDBRAIN

The hindbrain contains several important structures called the **medulla, cerebellum, and pons.** This portion of the brain is linked to the spine. There appears to be no distinctive separation between the spine and the hindbrain either in terms of structure or function.

The **medulla** contains many

spinal nerve tracts, and plays an important role in regulating breathing and circulation functions.

The **cerebellum** lies above and behind the medulla. It consists of two hemispheres containing larger numbers of nerve tissue connected to various regions in the brain. It plays an important role in regulating skeletal muscles and the general tone of the body. It also helps control equilibrium. Activities like walking that require extensive coordination also are controlled by this region of the brain.

The **pons** contains nerves that link the two main hemispheres of the brain together. It also carries nerve tracts to higher and lower regions of the brain.

THE MIDBRAIN

This area of the brain contains nerves connecting the cerebrum with the brain stem and spinal cord. It plays an important role in vision and hearing.

THE FOREBRAIN

The forebrain contains three principle sections called the **thalamus, limbic system, and the cerebrum.**

The **thalamus** is found just above the midbrain and plays a major role in relaying nervous impulses to receptors in various regions of the brain.

The **limbic system** is a complex of structures regulating a wide range of functions. Among the most important of these functions are emotions and various states of hunger and thirst.

The **cerebrum** contains two halves that are responsible for the higher level of thinking. The left side appears to control analytical and logical thinking, while the right side is primarily involved in abstract or creative thinking.

Step Two: Reading at Your Best Comprehension Rate

Before reading the text at your best comprehension rate, focus on your purpose while considering the type of information you require. Next, visualize the schematic information you obtained from skimming the text. Analyze, compare, and integrate the type of information you require with the information you know the text contains. With your mind focused, you can begin to read the text at your best comprehension rate.

Reading at your comprehension rate permits you to see the finer details of the text that you did not see during your previous skimming. Highlight these important details with additional lines and asterisks in the left margin. You still do not want to read slower in order to master extremely difficult information. Anything requiring an unusual amount of your reading time should be highlighted and reviewed during the third stage of reading for comprehension.

THE INNER VOICE

Avoid parroting the words in your text with your inner voice. Instead, use your inner voice to condense the information into short, schematically meaningful phrases that are easy to recall.

USING YOUR VARIOUS SENSES

While reading, visualize the text's information as if you were viewing it in a movie. Bring as many of your other senses as possible into the reading experience. Try to taste, touch, smell, feel, and hear what is being described by the words in the text. Every sense connects to different regions of your brain. The more regions you stimulate, the easier it is for you to remember important information.

ACTIVE READING

Frequently stop reading and ask the three types of questions described in Chapter One: literal, implied, and inferential. Difficulty in formulating questions is an indication that you do not fully understand the text.

If you read other books on the same subject, compare and contrast the information they contain with the data in your current text. Analyzing information requires using the brain's higher learning centers which increases both comprehension and recall of the material.

Step Three: Studying and Memorizing Specific Information

During the two previous steps, you left marks in the left margin to highlight important or difficult information contained in the text. Now is the time to return to these marks and master this data. Using the super-reading memory techniques described in this book, you can memorize any important concepts or definitions you require.

THE FOUR MOTIVES FOR READING

Analyzing all reasons for reading would reveal four primary motives. Each reading motive requires a different balance between comprehension, speed, and comfort. Although reading for comprehension using super reading may contain as many as three distinct steps, your reading motive determines how to use each step most efficiently. Use different strategies for each of the four types of reading: pleasure reading, hobby and special-interest reading, reading for studying, and reading to master information. Let us examine each of these strategies.

Mastering Strategies for Different Types of Reading: Pleasure Reading

During a television interview, Dick Cavett told me a wonderful story about his friend who several years ago took a different speed-reading program. During the introduction to this reading program, his teacher described how everyone would be able to use their new reading skill to master the important information in newspapers and magazines. He also told the students they would be able to speed quickly through inconsequential reading such as novels. Dick's friend loved novels. He enrolled in the speed reading class to develop an ability to read novels quickly. Disgusted by the teacher's put-down of fiction, Dick's friend left the speed-reading program.

Good for him. Learning to enjoy fiction at high speed should be a feature of any good speed-reading program. Fiction reading is an important form of pleasure reading. I would love to share with you my secrets for reading and enjoying fiction at high speed.

ENJOYING FICTION

Reading continues to be a popular form of relaxation. Pleasure reading involves no studying or memorization. It should be fun, entertaining, and relaxing. Good fiction offers us an escape from everyday life. Till now, the focus of this book has been primarily upon nonfiction. My lecturing experience has taught me that most speed-reading students use their skills for mastering nonfiction text. Still, many people want to use their super-reading skills to enjoy good fiction as well.

Do not perform productive skimming when reading fiction for pleasure. What pleasure can you derive from a novel if you know its ending before you begin reading the text at your comprehension rate? Probably very little. Pleasure reading requires no studying; your sole focus should be upon enjoyment. When reading fiction for a reason other than pleasure, you should use the techniques described in the sections Hobby and Special-Interest Reading, or Reading for Studying. During pleasure reading, you not only avoid productive skimming, you also avoid reviewing the book to learn specific details. In fact, the only reading comprehension step used for pleasure reading is the second step that requires you to read at your best comprehension rate.

Certain writers paint images with text that require you

to read slowly to savor the beauty of their words. I've commented in several newspapers that "reading Shakespeare at 80 pages per minute is like roller skating past art on a museum wall—you simply can not appreciate its beauty at high speed." If you enjoy classical literature or poetry, then you must read slowly enough to see and appreciate the individual words they contain. Super reading will help you dash through your other reading chores so you can find the extra time necessary for reading this type of text at the slower pace it deserves.

On *Morning Exchange,* a popular television program in Cleveland, I completed an 1,180 page book in under 20 minutes. The book was roughly the length of *Gone With The Wind.* However, you could not read *Gone With The Wind* in 20 minutes and still experience intense emotions. Imagine seeing Scarlet rejected after reading the book for 20 minutes. Your emotions simply could not react to the story's plot at that frantic pace. Although you still would comprehend the theme, plot, and character development, you would not experience its beauty. Reading fiction at top speed is like watching *Star Wars* on a VCR running on fast forward. Seeing the death star blow up after only viewing the movie for ten minutes would cause you to lose all the excitement of the picture.

The same thing happens when quickly reading good fiction. Unfortunately, few fiction writers have Shakespeare's genius for language, so it is possible to read their writing quickly without losing any enjoyment. I will soon describe certain modifications you can make in your reading that will enable you to read with increased speed while maintaining your enjoyment of the text.

The technique for reading fiction at high speed is

similar to the method used for obtaining comprehension during the second and third minute or your high-speed reading exercise. Remember how you maintained your comprehension when reading at double and triple your reading speed by varying your reading rate for different parts of a paragraph? This technique also enables you to read fiction at high speed without losing your enjoyment of the text.

The elements of a fiction text include plot, theme, atmosphere, and character development. Often, fiction authors write lengthy passages that you can easily speed through without missing any enjoyable text. If the atmosphere of a book takes up a large amount of text, double or triple your reading rate. Use topic sentences, verbs, and nouns to keep track of the flow of the text. By using these schematically rich sections of text, you will observe where there are interesting passages, so you can slow down to your comprehension rate to fully enjoy them. Varying your reading rate enables you to experience the emotional effects of a novel while keeping your average reading speed high.

I prefer to read nonfiction. Recently, I had the pleasure of reading an interesting fiction work, *The Mists of Avalon*, a wonderful novel about the knights of the Round Table told through the eyes of King Arthur's sister Morgan. This lengthy book contains long passages describing the atmosphere in King Arthur's court. In one passage, about five pages describe the appearance of King Arthur's throne room. Even if I read this information slowly, I would never remember all the detail it contained. In four seconds I completed these pages and my inner voice told me that ''it was a regal throne room.'' Similarly, the novel contained several pages describing Guinevere's dress. In one second, my inner voice told me that Guinevere had a ''stunning dress.'' Increasing my reading rate in these portions of the text actually enhanced my enjoyment of the book. I reached the other stimulating portions of the text quite quickly, and savored the story they contained.

Selectively reading fiction using the technique I just described is quite similar to how many people use their VCR to view a taped television movie. When viewing the movie, you use the fast-forward button to speed rapidly through the commercials. You would not enjoy the movie less because you did not spend time viewing every commercial message. Quite the opposite, you probably would find the movie more enjoyable without the annoying commercial interruptions. Slowly moving passages of fiction text can be as annoying as commercials interrupting a movie. By using your super-reading fiction strategy, you will finish more books in less time with greater enjoyment.

HOW TO STRUCTURE FICTION READING

Understanding text at high speed is usually not a problem. The difficulty with high-speed reading that most students experience is remembering the information they have read for more than a few seconds. The pages make sense while you read them, but after reading further you begin to forget what you have already read. This is a natural occurrence that can easily be overcome.

Imagine that each bit of information the text contains is a small, colored marble. Information belonging to the same category has the same color. For example, the plot marbles are the same color, as are the theme marbles, and so on. In your mind, set up different colored jars, each of which will hold marbles of the same color. You will have jars for the plot, theme, atmosphere, and various characters. During high-speed reading, place the information into its appropriately colored jar. Using an organized method to view the text's information makes it easier for your mind to comprehend and retain it.

Your brain likes storing information in this organized fashion. Instead of using marbles in jars, imagine your brain contains folders labeled *plot, theme, atmosphere,* and *character names*. During reading, place each bit of information in its proper folder. Suddenly, the deluge of information becomes an organized flow you can easily follow at high speed.

READING NEWSPAPERS AND MAGAZINES FOR PLEASURE

Remembering information in newspapers and magazines is easy to accomplish by using a different set of mental folders to hold the information. This type of text needs folders labeled *who, what, where, when, why,* and *how*. Journalists are trained to offer information using these key questions to organize the flow of text. At high speed, your eyes search for the information corresponding to these questions. When you spot a piece of this information, instantly file it in its appropriate folder.

Zipping through magazines and newspapers will help you stay current with what is happening in the world and can help you achieve the success you deserve. You can complete the Sunday *Times* in less than an hour by scanning each of the sections to find articles important to your needs. Once you locate these articles, you can read them again at your comprehension rate to memorize the information.

Hobby and Special-Interest Reading

Reading is the key to learning how to accomplish things of interest to you. Hobby and special-interest reading require some learning, but no one is going to test your understanding of the information except you. Special-interest reading of this type requires the use of all three reading comprehension steps.

Productively skim your book to learn about its schema and layout. Does your book contain sections or features with special information you can quickly obtain? Are there summaries, graphs, diagrams, or other features you can use? Your motive for reading the book should be clearly known to you while reading. Search for areas of the text containing the information directly related to this motive.

During the second step, read your book at your best comprehension rate. Again, look for information related to your reading purpose. Increase your speed when the author presents schematic information not related to your needs, and slow down when you perceive important details. Continue marking the margin of the text to highlight important facts that need to be comprehended or memorized.

Once you complete your comprehension reading, return to the highlighted text to study and memorize key facts and concepts. Since you are reading for a personal goal, you may not need to study a great deal of information. You often may obtain the details you require during your comprehension reading.

I frequently use this technique to learn new computer programs. Using this method, I learned how to use *Wordstar* and *WordPerfect* in under three hours. So can you! First, I skimmed the program's book at high speed to find out how the information was distributed. Then, reading at my best comprehension rate, I learned what the program could do for me. I did not stop to learn the details of how to perform all the functions. All I wanted to know was what kinds of functions I could perform with the software. Once I knew what the software was capable of doing, I began to run the program on my computer. I read the book only to learn the functions necessary for me to start using the software. When my work required a specialized function, I knew from my reading that the software could perform it. Then I returned to the text to master that specific program function. Instead of spending weeks reading the program manual, I learned in minutes what I needed to immediately use the program. Often, all you require when reading for hobby and special-interest purposes is an awareness of how a skill is performed. When your purpose requires greater detail, simply return to the text to master the skill on a deeper level.

Studying

Usually, reading for the purpose of studying requires learning information you will not need to retain for the rest of your life, but need to know temporarily in detail. You study to fulfill someone else's expectations. That someone else might be an employer, client, or instructor. What they expect you to learn is far more important than any information that may be of interest to you.

Begin studying with a productive skimming of the book. Never spend more than 15 minutes scanning the complete text. The majority of your time should be spent learning the information the text contains, and not learning about the text. Using the suggestions made earlier in this chapter, skim to acquire information contained in the book's features at high speed. The table of contents is an exception, and should be read at your comprehension rate. The schema it contains is worth taking some extra moments to learn. In a large text, skimming three to five chapters is sufficient. If the book's format contains units holding several chapters, be certain to skim at least one unit. It is also important to watch for any summaries in the book. Highlight important places in the text by using lines and asterisks.

When reading for comprehension, look for the information related to your learning objective. Continue highlighting the text, including passages that require more time for you to comprehend.

Too often, students equate reading with studying. Studying is learning, memorizing, and comprehending information. Reading inputs information into the brain. When studying, use high-speed reading to locate important information, and then spend 50 to 70 percent of your time learning it. This is the third step in the comprehension process. Reading should take only a small percentage of your total study time.

Reading to Master Information

You should be able to master information that must be remembered for long periods of time in minute detail. For example, lawyers can't tell a judge they meant to object yesterday in court. Pilots can't almost know when to put down the landing gear. Doctors can't almost remember how to perform the next step of an operation. These people must remember everything from their training, and be able to remember important information instantly throughout their entire lives. Mastering information can often be a life-and-death issue.

Reading to master information means that you must use most of your time learning rather than reading. Once you locate the pertinent facts, your time should be spent memorizing and comprehending them. Only 10 percent of your time should be spent reading, and the other 90 percent should be spent learning.

The first step in mastering information requires productive skimming. Pay attention to any visual aids like tables or diagrams that can help you comprehend the text. Mark off important passages of text. During the second phase of mastering information, read at your best comprehension rate, continuing to highlight important passages of text that need to be mastered. Finally, spend the majority of your time memorizing and learning your highlighted information.

HOW TO COMPREHEND LENGTHY TECHNICAL MATERIAL

"How do you eat an elephant?" is a question often asked in beginning writing classes. The answer is simple:

"One bite at a time." Mastering lengthy technical text requires the same simple logic. Break up the lengthy text into small easy-to-learn chunks. In this way, your mind never has to learn more information than it can comfortably devour.

First, skim the entire text at top speed. As always, pay attention to the index, glossary, table of contents, and other features to determine how familiar the material appears to you.

Next, read the first chapter at high speed. During this step, determine how far you can read before you begin to forget the information. This amount will vary in different texts according to your background, aptitude, and understanding of their schemata. Remember, your objective during this step is to determine how far you can read with comprehension before you start forgetting text. You are not yet trying to comprehend the information.

As a result of these two steps, you have an understanding of both the text and the difficulty level of the current chapter. You can see how the books fit together and the role the current chapter plays in the schema of the entire text. Begin to break down the chapter into the easy-to-learn chunks you selected. In some texts, the chunk may be as large as the entire chapter. In other texts, the chunk's size may be a page, a section printed in boldface type, or even a single paragraph.

Go to your first chunk and perform each of the three steps for obtaining reading comprehension. First, skim it at high speed to determine its general content, and mark off important definitions and concepts in the margin. Then, read the information at your best comprehension rate, continuing to mark off the important sections in the left margin. Finally, spend the bulk of your time memorizing and learning the information that is marked off in the text. When done, move to the next chunk and repeat these three steps until all the chunks in the chapter are complete.

EXTRA FAST READING

Often, your reading will require an awareness of only key information in a text. When you need to be familiar with only the contents of a text, it is possible to read at very high speed with good comprehension. Using your double or triple reading rate, look for the topic sentences, verbs and nouns, and passages of text containing schema. Read the text only one time to obtain an understanding of the who, what, where, when, why, and how of a topic. This type of reading enables you to learn about a great many things without getting slowed down by details. If, after reading, you decide some of the details are important, return to them in the highlighted parts of the text and learn them.

Summary

1. The steps used in reading for comprehension are skimming, reading, and studying.
2. Productive skimming enables you to quickly scan through a text to learn about its schema, and should take only two to five seconds per page.
3. To retain information, use as many of your senses as possible during reading.
4. There are four motives for reading: pleasure, hobbies and special interest, studying, and mastering information.

5. Organizing information when reading at high speed makes it easier for your brain to comprehend and retain it.

6. You can read text in one step if your goal is only to become aware of its key points.

CHAPTER SIX

Learning to Study Effectively

GOALS

- UNDERSTANDING THE FOUR
  INFORMATION LEVELS
- LEARNING HOW TO DETERMINE THE
  APPROPRIATE LEVEL OF INFORMATION
- USING AWARENESS-LEVEL
  INFORMATION
- USING FAMILIARITY-LEVEL INFORMATION
- USING KNOWLEDGE-LEVEL
  INFORMATION
- USING EXPERTISE-LEVEL INFORMATION
- LEARNING HOW TO DETERMINE WHAT
  TO STUDY FOR SCHOOL
- LEARNING HOW TO DETERMINE WHAT
  TO STUDY FOR BUSINESS
- LEARNING HOW TO USE SCHEMATIC
  MAPPING

HOW TO DETERMINE WHAT TO STUDY

Few people enjoy taking exams, and almost all people have experienced difficulty taking an examination at some time in their lives. Despite the fact that you prepare, there is still the possibility of studying the wrong information. Wouldn't it be wonderful if you could predetermine what information a supervisor, client, or instructor expects you to know? This would enable you to succeed not only in the classroom, but more importantly, achieve your career goals. Fortunately, you can determine what others expect you to learn from books. This chapter will describe the secrets for studying the correct material.

THE FOUR INFORMATION LEVELS

Just as reading has four motives, there are four levels on which you can learn information: awareness, familiarity, knowledge, or expertise. To raise your knowledge of a subject from one level to the next requires investing both time and effort.

Reading for a personal goal makes it easy to choose which information to learn. You find the book containing information on your particular level, locate this information in text at high speed, and then study it. When we study to fulfill the expectations of someone else, we must first determine their priorities in order to study the correct information. Often, people study information on the wrong level. Choosing a level that is too difficult wastes time and often results in missing important details. It is essential to be able to recognize at high speed the knowledge level of each fact.

How to Determine the Appropriate Level
of Information

It is easy to learn how to recognize the various levels of information. As a sample subject, I picked organic chemistry because it is a complex subject containing a wide range of information. It will be easy for you to develop a full awareness of the four levels by observing how they function in organic chemistry.

Awareness-Level Information

Knowing the fundamental principles of a subject is the awareness level of information. A fundamental concept in organic chemistry is the nuclear magnetic resonance spectrum or NMRS. That's a pretty formidable sounding concept, but it has a very simple meaning. A nuclear magnetic resonance spectrum is an electronic fingerprint of an organic compound.

Let us take a quick quiz on the information you just learned about nuclear magnetic resonance spectrums. Don't think you know much about the subject? It doesn't matter when the question is asked on the awareness level. "True or false, a nuclear magnetic resonance spectrum is an electronic fingerprint of an organic compound?" See how simple it is to master information on the awareness level? It only took a second to learn what seemed very difficult.

Knowing about a nuclear magnetic resonance spectrum on only the awareness level, you couldn't either recognize or interpret one even if it was given to you. When studying, if you decide that the awareness level of understanding information is insufficient for your needs, you can always return to the text to learn the information on a higher level. Mark off this important text, and return to it when you have more reading time available. By reading at the awareness level, you will be able to read huge amounts of text in a short period of time. This will not only broaden your understanding of life, it may also help you find important information that you previously missed.

Awareness-level information takes an instant to learn, and is easy to spot even at a high reading speed. Awareness-level understanding is often all that is required when reading text for relaxation. It works perfectly when reading newspapers, magazines, business journals, and letters at high speed. Reading these texts at top speed, you obtain information about the latest occurrences from a wide variety of sources.

Exercise

Choose a novel and read it at the awareness level. Practice varying your reading speed to derive the maximum benefit of speed and pleasure.

Familiarity-Level Information

The main categories of a subject are understood on the familiarity level of information. Continuing to use organic chemistry as an example, you will find that organic compounds are arranged in groupings similar to biological organisms. You wouldn't have much difficulty recognizing the differences between a fish, reptile, bird, or mammal, nor would an organic chemist have difficulty distinguishing between the primary nuclear magnetic resonance spectrums of common organic compound groupings. It might take several days to learn the major characteristics of the different organic compounds displayed on a nuclear magnetic resonance spectrum. This is longer than it took to learn the definition of this level. Since it takes longer to learn information on each successive level, when learning a subject on the familiarity level, more time will be required than when learning on the awareness level.

Hobby and special-interest reading is typically performed on the familiarity level of understanding. You use it to learn the specific information that is required to accomplish a task. Sometimes it is not necessary to know every detail contained in a text to complete an objective. When this happens, learn data related to your primary objective and read the rest of the text on the awareness level.

Exercise

1. Learn a new skill from a nonfiction book by reading it on the familiarity level as suggested above.
2. Skim the material quickly to learn about the book's format and key points.
3. Read the book at your comprehension rate, marking off key points with lines and asterisks in the margin.
4. Study the key points you need to remember.

Knowledge-Level Information

The main examples belonging to each category are the focus of reading of information on the knowledge-level.

Let's continue to use organic chemistry to illustrate this principle in action. Each of the main organic groupings contains about 100 compounds. Most of the time, they are chemicals you would see on your nuclear magnetic resonance spectrums in a laboratory. If you viewed thousands of NMRSs, possibly 95 percent of them would contain one of these compounds.

Learning to identify the characteristics of these common chemicals might take several months to a year. Once you have learned these characteristics, you then would be able to perform an analysis of most compounds brought into the lab.

The knowledge level of reading commonly requires you to have some previous knowledge of a subject. It requires more time to master information on this level than it takes to learn information on the familiarity level. Fortunately, we study information related to our primary interests and professions as a matter of course. As we develop schemata in these areas, it becomes easier to develop new knowledge by drawing upon what we already know.

Exercise

1. Choose a textbook on a subject that you find interesting.
2. Skim the book at high speed to discover its schema.
3. Read the book at your best comprehension rate to learn the details.
4. Highlight important and confusing text by placing lines and asterisks in the left margin.
5. Study the highlighted passages of text.

Expertise-Level Information

Understanding knowledge on the expertise level requires a complete understanding of all the major points and subdivisions of a discipline with no room for error. There are thousands of nuclear magnetic resonance spectrums you could obtain in a lab. A police scientist must be able to pinpoint every chemical found in the evidence from a crime scene. Using a mud sample taken from a shoe, a police lab must precisely determine the original location of the mud. Getting this precision from a nuclear magnetic resonance spectrum requires years of training, plus a considerable aptitude for learning this information. At the expertise level, aptitude is an important factor in determining if you are capable of mastering a subject area.

Expertise-level information calls for the total recall of every concept, major category, and the prime examples belonging to each category. Often, it requires knowing minute details. Doctors, lawyers, pilots, and other professionals are among those individuals who must comprehend and retain extensive amounts of information. Usually, it takes a lifetime to master information on the expertise level in certain fields.

With time and practice, expertise-level information becomes less difficult to learn. A person who has spent years studying organic chemistry in an advanced degree program would use this technical expertise-level information on a regular basis. Eventually, it becomes part of the person's working knowledge. The complexity of information is a relative concept dependent on how much experience you have working in a subject area. Information that might be challenging to a layman is common knowledge for an expert. Consequently, the expert requires less time to learn new data. This extra experience makes learning complicated information easier.

Before starting to read, you must know how to find the level of information you need. We'll begin by investigating how college students can predetermine what level of information they should learn in a course. Then we'll examine how to determine the appropriate learning level for other situations that require intensive studying.

Exercise

1. Choose a detailed book on a subject related to your occupation.
2. Skim the book at high speed to learn about its format.
3. Read the book at your best comprehension rate, and highlight the details with lines and asterisks in the margin.
4. Instead of reading the material, spend 90 percent of your time learning the highlighted information.

HOW TO DETERMINE WHAT TO STUDY FOR SCHOOL

Inspecting old examinations kept on file at a college is one of the easiest ways to determine the level of information a professor expects you to learn. Few students look at these old examinations, and the few who do often foolishly expect the same questions to appear on all upcoming examinations. Instead, you should study old examinations with the intent of analyzing the percentage of questions occurring on each of the learning levels just discussed. Is the professor asking questions about key points, main categories, primary groupings within a category, or is the professor asking for very specific information? The percentage of questions on each of these levels on prior tests will be consistent with the percentages found on the upcoming test. Once you determine the percentage of information on each learning level, you can look for any information in your text and lecture notes on each level. Spend the majority of your time studying this information, and don't waste time learning material that is on a higher level than what is likely to be included in test questions. Higher-level information may be important for obtaining an understanding of the subject, but it is totally unrelated to scoring high marks on upcoming examinations. You can choose to learn this information at another time when your purpose is unrelated to passing an examination. Studying to get high marks is different from studying to learn a subject.

If your school doesn't keep old examinations on file, try to obtain previous examinations from someone who took the course with the same teacher. Sometimes you cannot even find a friend who possesses an old examination. If this occurs, obtain sample tests from other professors in the same department of the college. Schools tend to encourage teachers to create exams that use a similar difficulty level; however, using a sample test from a different professor is less reliable than using one from your own.

The amount of time a professor spends on a topic is an indication of the emphasis that will be placed on it when making up an examination. If you have a difficult textbook but the professor talks primarily about information on a knowledge or familiarity level, you can be relatively certain the professor does not expect you to master the textbook information. If the professor did, more class time would be spent discussing it. If your book is relatively easy but the professor spends time on very difficult topics, you can expect a considerable portion of your examination to contain more difficult questions. Use your professor's time allocation to subjects in class as a barometer that measures the relative weight that will be given to the same material on exams. If you have managed to obtain old tests, you can determine if your hypothesis is true by looking at the types of questions on the old tests and the proportion of time these topics occupied during lectures.

There is a paradox in academic studying. Students read texts to acquire knowledge, but they also must obtain high grades. These two purposes sometimes conflict with each other. Certain professors are excellent educators, but tend to give low grades. They expect you to learn information on the expertise level in lower-level classes. This is not a reasonable expectation, and can cost you dearly. When attending undergraduate school, your most important purpose is to get the high grades necessary for gaining entrance into a prestigious graduate program. A prestigious graduate program will help ensure your future success far more than your undergraduate degree. Unfortunately, this may require you at times to learn from professors who give easier exams, rather than from those who are excellent teachers. Ideally, these two qualities will be found in the same individual—often they are not.

I learned this lesson from bitter experience while

attending undergraduate college. In my vertebrate zoology class, one student averaged 82 percent, I averaged 78 percent, and everyone else had averages in the teens and single digits. The professor gave a *B* to the student with the 82-percent average, gave me a *C*, and failed 16 other students. Although on the curve I scored an *A+*, my professor elected not to grade the class in this manner. As a result, I had a *C* on my transcript which actually represented *A* work in that class. Unfortunately, transcripts do not carry footnotes to explain the relative significance of grades. Learn from my mistake, and don't remain in a class with a teacher who does not give you a fair opportunity to earn your grade.

Unfortunately, at that time I didn't possess the knowledge of how to take tests that I now have. Several years ago, I had the opportunity to try my test strategies for mastering technical information on an advanced placement examination on educational psychology. New York State offers college credits if you can pass a multiple-choice examination on a topic. You study by yourself using only a textbook. There are no classes, teachers, or assignments to help you. At that time, I was temporarily teaching school in New York City, and needed the college credits to keep my job.

Having a busy schedule, I forgot about the test. Looking at my appointment book on a Sunday evening, I was horrified to discover the test was scheduled for the coming Friday, and I hadn't even purchased the textbook! The next morning I ran to the bookshop, intending to buy a review book on the subject that would make my studying easier. I searched in vain for this review book; instead, I had to purchase the 700-page textbook suggested by the state. More importantly, I had a week filled with appointments and only seven hours of study time available.

Failing this test meant losing my job. I used my studying strategies to learn the information. First, I asked myself what kinds of questions would the individuals preparing the examination be most likely to ask. They would consider the student population taking the exam. That was an easy question to answer. The students taking the test could be anyone in the state of New York wanting college credit in educational psychology. This meant that the majority of the test questions would be on the familiarity and knowledge levels of information. The examiners couldn't ask questions on the awareness level because the questions would be too easy. Everyone would get the correct answers and the examiners would lose their jobs. The examiners couldn't ask questions on the expertise level because that would be too hard. Many people would incorrectly answer the questions, and many complaints would be sent to the state about the difficulty of the test. I counted on the examiners wanting to stay employed, and concluded that the majority of the exam questions would be on the familiarity and knowledge levels. The state informed us that the questions would use a multiple-choice format—meaning that all I had to do was recognize the correct answer from among several choices.

Before starting to study, I asked myself, why am I reading the text? What is my purpose? Was it to learn about educational psychology? No! I was taking the exam to get four college credits in order to keep my job. Passing the test was my purpose, not learning the material. With this in mind, I knew that important information about educational psychology would not appear on the exam, so I could safely skip studying any items that were on an inappropriate learning level along with any extremely hard or easy material. Also, information that wouldn't fit into a multiple-choice test would be missing. If my purpose was to learn about educational psychology, the focus of my reading would be quite different than the focus I would need to pass a test on educational psychology.

First, I read the book at high speed to locate any material I learned while studying psychology in college. It only took about twenty minutes to complete this stage of my study.

I knew that information on the familiarity and knowledge levels would be used in the largest portion of the questions, so I studied this type of data for about one and a half hours.

Next, I started studying the difficult material. I knew that most of it would take too long for me to learn. Since it was so highly technical, it was unlikely to be heavily represented on the test, so I wasn't concerned about learning much of it. Expertise-level information is often demanding, and would not make up a large proportion of the questions. I deliberately skipped several concepts that I found difficult and that would have taken several hours to learn, focusing instead on several topics that I could study in that same time period.

Finally, I spent time studying the glossary. In any multiple-choice examination, many of the questions will be word-identification ones, and the glossary contains most of the definitions for these words. The glossary was quite long. Far too lengthy for me to study in the remaining time. However, many of the definitions were either too easy or too difficult. It was unlikely they would appear on the exam. Other material I already knew from my prior studies and didn't need to study. I only needed to learn three pages of new word meanings that were likely to appear on the exam.

At last the moment of truth came. I completed the four-hour test in under 50 minutes. Almost 60 percent of the test consisted of the vocabulary words I had studied. The rest of the exam focused upon information on the familiarity and knowledge levels that I expected to see.

The test was graded on a curve used to evaluate students who had taken the same test after completing a semester of educational psychology. These students had a professor, took exams, wrote reports, and had regular homework assignments. To complete a four-month college program in seven hours, and then receive a $B+$ when compared to this group is an excellent testimonial of how well super reading works under demanding conditions.

HOW TO DETERMINE WHAT TO STUDY FOR BUSINESS

Studying for school is only one reason for studying. Many businesses require people to learn new material on a regular basis. In these instances, you do not have past exams to guide your study. However, there are many things you can do to prepare for meetings with clients or supervisors that will help you become a master reader. The secret to mastering business studies is to analyze the past performances of clients and supervisors. In this section, we shall examine some of the potential situations you may encounter, and how to master them.

New Job—Old Client

Suppose a client for whom you have previously worked returns to have you bid on a project that lies outside of your area of expertise. Analyze the level of information the client sought from you during past sales presentations. Were most of the questions asked on the familiarity level, or did the client typically ask a great deal of expertise-level questions? Remember that for someone regularly performing complex work, the expertise level of competency may actually become their familiarity level. Make certain that you do not overprepare yourself by studying information on the level other than the one the client characteristically expects you to know. Not only will your client be satisfied with your presentation, but your productivity will also increase because of your new learning efficiency.

New Client—Old Job

Here the scenario changes a bit. You are working with a new client on a project you've performed for others in the past. Analyze the type of questions others typically ask on this subject. What learning level do these questions belong to? If you have several clients who expect you to know material on the knowledge level, and suddenly a client requests only expertise-level information from you, you may want to reconsider having them as a client.

Clients that take up more time than others may not be worth having as clients. If one client requires more than double the time of another without bringing in additional funds, you should give serious consideration to dismissing that client. Cultivate clients who use your time productively.

New Job—New Client

This is the most difficult scenario of all. In it, you lack experience with both the job and the client. Have faith, there are still many things you can do to prepare for this common situation.

First, ask yourself if you have any friends in your industry who have experience doing the type of work you are about to undertake. Ask them what questions their clients have typically asked about this work.

Another good place to get information on new clients and new work is through professional groups and associations. Ask them to refer you to others who have experience with the type of work you are about to perform or to anyone familiar with your new client.

Before attempting to study any information, it is important for you to know as much as possible about the job you are undertaking. In doing this, you are obtaining the schema of the project. Once you start reading, you can easily identify the information related to your specific needs.

HOW TO USE SCHEMATIC MAPPING

Traditional outlining has many limitations. Once you have started to arrange information in a particular order, it is difficult to add new information or make changes. If after making your outline, you see a relationship between two items that you would like to change, it is very difficult to accomplish this using a traditional outline. You have to renumber and reletter most of the entries—a time-consuming procedure. Most learning experts now recommend the use of schematic maps when taking notes on detailed information.

Schematic mapping works in harmony with how your creative mind functions. It is more visual than traditional outlining and often uses a treelike image to help organize information. In schematic mapping, lines are drawn which lead to a central theme. Subdivisions are included as additional lines on a primary branch. In this manner you can see the relationships that exist between various ideas as they relate to a central premise. Schematic mapping is ideally suited for making changes and viewing different types of information quickly and without confusion. Let's take a moment to practice making a simple schematic map of a brief essay about the flow of blood through the body.

Exercise

Read the passage about blood flow and make a schematic map containing the main information.

THE HEART

The heart is a muscular organ whose rhythmic contractions push blood through the circulatory system. About the size of a fist and located in the center of the chest, it is made primarily from cardiac muscle cells.

These muscle cells interlock with each other in a pattern that is not found in any other muscle in the body.

The pericardium is a strong membrane that surrounds the outside of the heart. Inside, the heart is divided into four chambers. The two upper chambers are called auricles, while the two lower chambers are called ventricles.

Deoxygenated blood enters the heart through the right auricle, a chamber located in the upper right-hand portion of the heart. This small chamber forces the blood downward into the right ventricle. The contractions of the right ventricle move the blood into the lungs. While in the lungs, the blue-colored blood releases its carbon dioxide and absorbs oxygen. It returns to the left auricle on the upper left-hand portion of the heart. The oxygenated blood is now colored dark red. The small left auricle passes the blood into the left ventricle, the largest chamber in the heart. Located on the lower left, the left ventricle is responsible for pumping blood to all the tissues in the body. It is the largest chamber in the heart.

Very technical topics may require several diagrams before you're able to grasp the finer points. One of the spokes on a schematic diagram may become the circle for another diagram. Similarly, it is possible to take one of the branches on a diagram and make it the main trunk of another diagram. Each of these new diagrams then has a more specific focus and will encompass more details about a topic. This process is similar to using a micro-

Our schematic map of the heart will describe the main chambers and the condition of the blood flowing through them. Begin by drawing a circular figure and call it the heart. You can label this figure by indicating the top and bottom, left and right sides. The auricles are located on top, and the ventricles are located on the bottom. Now label the left side and the right side by drawing a line that divides the diagram in half. Now label the various chambers by drawing lines indicating their proper names. Let's do this as an exercise together.

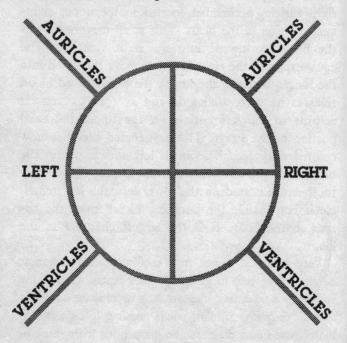

For a different example, let's use the subject of ancient history. This topic includes China, the Fertile Crescent, and Europe. Each of these items appears as a single line around a circle called ancient history. Now you can form a circle and call it the Fertile Crescent. On that circle you can list the various civilizations associated with that time period as shown on the accompanying diagram.

Next, you can form a circle that highlights one of these civilizations. Let's use a circle that highlights ancient Europe. Now we are using the middle power of our schematic technique.

Going to high power, we can highlight one of these lines as a central idea, and surround it with considerable detail.

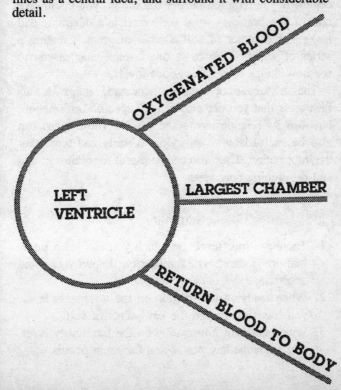

scope under different powers. Under low power, you can see the entire specimen but without much detail. Medium power has more detail, but you see a smaller portion of the specimen. Under high power, you see only a small area of the specimen, but with excellent detail.

To continue this analogy, by using low power we can see the anatomy of the entire heart. It is easy to see the relationships that exist between the primary chambers of the heart at this level of magnification. Suppose you needed more detail about the left ventricle. You could draw another diagram placing the left ventricle at the center. If you required greater resolution, you could take one of the branches from the ventricle's diagram, and make it the center of still another diagram. Creating a series of schematic maps in this fashion enables you to see how things relate on various levels.

The advantage of creating schematic maps in this fashion is that you not only see the specific information, but also its relationship to the whole. These maps can also be useful later when trying to study and remember the information. They also can be useful for brainstorming and developing new ideas.

Summary

1. There are four levels on which you can learn information: awareness, familiarity, knowledge, and expertise.
2. When studying information on the awareness level, you focus only upon the key points of text.
3. When studying information on the familiarity level, you learn the key points and the main details.

4. When studying information on the knowledge level, you learn the key points, main supportive details, and examples for each of the main supportive details.

5. When studying information on the expertise levels, you must be familiar with all information related to a topic.

6. Examine old exams and your lecture notes to become aware of what level of information will turn up on an examination.

7. When trying to perform unfamiliar work for an old client, keep in mind the level of information the client typically expects you to know when bidding on a job.

8. When trying to perform familiar work for a new client, analyze the levels of questions other clients typically asked you before you started to work for them.

9. When trying to perform unfamiliar work for a new client, contact groups and individuals who can tell you what types of questions clients typically ask about this work. Also try to find out as much information as possible about your new client's preferences.

10. Schematic maps help you spatially organize information. They are easier to rearrange than traditional outlines.

CHAPTER SEVEN

How to Develop
a Super Memory

GOALS

- INDEXING YOUR MEMORY
- PEGGING INFORMATION TO YOUR BODY
- USING THE POWER OF MUSIC TO
  DEVELOP A SUPER MEMORY
- USING MUSIC TO OVERCOME BOREDOM
  WHEN STUDYING
- CLUSTERING INFORMATION
- USING LEARNING SETS
- USING ENVELOPES TO TEST YOUR
  MEMORY
- MEMORIZING A SCRIPT
- GETTING YOUR THREE MEMORIES TO
  WORK TOGETHER
- REMEMBERING WHAT YOU STUDY

You possess an infallible memory, one that even re-
members songs and nursery rhymes from childhood.

When you are having trouble recalling facts, you may find it hard to believe that your memory is infallible. Your memory is perfect, it is recalling information that can sometimes be a problem. For example, you meet someone you haven't seen in a long time in a store, but you can't remember the person's name. How embarrassing. A few days later in the middle of the night, you suddenly wake up and remember it. It is not that the person's name was forgotten, it's just that you couldn't recall the name when you needed it.

Retaining and recalling information obtained during high-speed reading is a critical skill that every super reader must master. This chapter teaches you how to develop a powerful memory, one that will enable you to make full use of all the information you have derived from a text.

INDEXING YOUR MEMORY

My favorite memorization method is to use index cards to summarize the key points found in a text. There are two types of information you will want to remember from your reading: concepts and definitions. *Concepts* describe how or why something works. A good example of a concept is the first law of motion found in physics. It states, "An object at rest tends to remain at rest until acted upon by an outside force." Although concepts may vary from one subject to another, they always will describe the operation of a particular principle. Concepts may be found at the literal, implied, or even the inferential level of meaning in a text.

Definitions are the literal meanings in a text. Names, dates, formulas, places, and anything that must be specifically recalled can be a definition. When learning a foreign language, you must memorize thousands of important definitions. An example of a definition is the meaning of the Spanish word *hola;* it means "hello" in English. Remembering this meaning is a simple act of memorization.

For five years I taught in the New York City school system and saw how many students did not understand the information they were taught. You could teach students concepts, but if you asked either inferential or implied questions, many of them were unable to give the correct answers. They performed well only when they had to repeat a bit of memorized literal information. It is important not only to memorize information, but also to understand how to apply it. The active reading process helps accomplish this objective. Creating questions while reading causes your brain to think critically about the information's deeper significance.

How to Use Index Cards

Keep a separate set of index cards for each subject you want to study. Don't mix language index cards with science index cards. To make an index card for learning a definition, write the meaning on one side and the key phrase on the other. To make an index card for learning a concept, write the concept on one side and the key phrase on the other.

Studies performed by psychologists indicate that you must shuffle the index cards into a random order before studying them. Otherwise, you may only be able to recall the facts on the index cards in their original order.

Psychologists call this phenomenon place learning. For example, if you memorize state capitals you would want to be able to recall the state capital of Michigan without having to recall all of the other state capitals that precede it in alphabetical order. Shuffling the index cards eliminates the problem of place learning by forcing the brain to learn each individual index card's meaning rather than the index card's place in alphabetical order.

Imagine that you are using index cards to study Spanish. After shuffling the deck, you look at the back of the first index card and it says "hello." After thinking for a moment, you say the answer aloud: *hola*. Since you correctly identified the definition, place the card on a completed pile, and continue with the next one. However, if you incorrectly identified the definition, you can use some super-reading tricks to train your brain to remember this information.

Identifying the meanings of words by looking at an index card uses only your visual sense. Your brain can store information by using a variety of senses. You are probably not even conscious of using some senses to store information. Have you ever tried to spell a word by saying it aloud, only to find you could not remember its spelling? Writing it down with a pen, you could easily recall how to spell the same word. Didn't it seem strange that a word you could not spell by speaking was suddenly easy to spell because you wrote it? There is a very important reason for this phenomenon. The part of your brain retaining spelling information is not directly linked to your speech center. In fact, you almost never spell words while talking. When do you always have to spell words? When writing! As a result, the brain's motor

center which controls the movement of your writing hand
retains a memory of how words are spelled. Using this
motor center, you can recall important information about
spelling that is unavailable to your mind's speech center.

Observe how your brain is capable of using many
regions to store important information. When experiencing difficulty recalling information using your visual
sense, you will want to master this information by using
all your senses. This helps ensure a quick recall of the
information when needed.

It is easy to train your other senses to retain information if you make a mistake about a concept or definition
written on one of your index cards. Take a legal-size
writing pad and write the concept or definition that you
incorrectly identified 25 times. Saying the concept or
definition aloud while writing it down has a profound
influence on many regions of your brain.

The visual region of your brain records the information, but you are also storing the information in other
regions that previously were ignored. The motor centers
connected to your writing hand store the information.
Speaking the information aloud stores the information in
the motor centers connected to your vocal chords, tongue,
and lips, as well as stimulating your ears and the regions
of the brain controlling hearing. More regions of your
brain will actively store important information when
using this technique.

Place any index cards you have incorrectly identified
on a pile separate from the index cards that you have
correctly identified. When you have finished testing yourself on each index card, return to the index cards you
have incorrectly identified and shuffle them. This ensures

a new random order to these index cards. Again, test your recall of these index cards. If you make a mistake, again write down the correct answer 25 times while speaking it aloud. Place the index cards you have correctly identified on the completed pile, and practice repeatedly the meanings of the other index cards until you can correctly identify all of them. Using this technique, you eventually will remember the most difficult concepts and definitions.

Repeatedly writing down and saying definitions aloud is so annoying that your brain will prefer to remember the information rather than going through the process again.

Get into the habit of using the index cards on a regular basis. During every study session, place the new index cards into your deck. It won't matter that your pile of index cards may grow quite large. Only the index cards you don't know will present a challenge, while the majority of the index cards will be instantly recalled because of your constant study. The only index cards requiring your time will be the ones added that day, or older ones that you have forgotten and need to relearn.

Continually practicing with the entire index-card deck helps prevent certain problems commonly experienced by students and professionals. Students taking finals often forget the information learned at the beginning of a term. Using my method, students will review the entire semester's work throughout the term. They do not have to work hard to remember this information for a final. The studying is done on a regular schedule so that even a large number of index cards can be reviewed in a very short amount of time. Professionals preparing for meetings and presentations can review key facts written on index cards, ensuring a perfect recall of the pertinent details when they are needed. No more waiting till the last minute to intensively study material. Your familiarity with your material is complete, making you relaxed and confident throughout your presentation.

Using Emotion to Heighten Retention

Think of a truly frightening movie. The director used visual and auditory effects to trick your imagination into believing the actions you saw were real. You also can trick your brain into retaining more information in a text by using more of your senses while reading. Try to experience the information in a text as if it were actually happening to you. When studying American history, visualize George Washington crossing the Delaware River. Feel the gnawing cold, smell the water, and taste the air as it bites into your face. Using vivid imagery makes it easier to recall this information later.

Even relatively dull information like chemistry can involve your senses during reading. See experiments being performed in your imagination rather than simply reading about them. When possible, focus all your senses as you attempt to memorize the details in a text. Later, while recalling information, the images your brain forms during your study session will trigger your memory.

Exercise

This exercise gives you practice creating index cards for memorizing important information.

1. Obtain a stack of 3″ × 5″ index cards, and write

down each of the words and their definitions from the list of biological definitions shown below.

2. Shuffle the index cards, and read the word(s) appearing on one side of the index card.

3. Attempt to recall the information written on the other side of the index card.

4. If you correctly identify the information, place the index card on the completed pile.

5. If you incorrectly identify the information, write down the correct answer 25 times while speaking it aloud. Place this index card on a pile with the other index cards you have incorrectly identified.

6. Once you have completed the entire pile, repeat steps 1 through 5 with the pile of index cards you have incorrectly identified. Continue until all the index cards have been completely memorized.

BIOLOGICAL DEFINITIONS

SIDE ONE	SIDE TWO
osmosis	diffusion of sugar through a membrane
cells	the smallest living unit
tissues	a grouping of cells having a similar function
organ	a grouping of tissues having a similar function
chromosome	structure found in the nucleus of a cell that contains the genetic material

chloroplast	part of a plant cell containing chlorophyll
ribosome	part of cell responsible for the manufacture of proteins
mitochondria	the structure in the cell where energy is liberated for performing life functions
pharynx	the throat
runner	horizontal stem with buds that takes part in vegetative reproduction
liver	organ secreting bile, an important digestive enzyme
neuron	a cell that transmits nervous impulses
petal	one of the leaflike structures of a flower
pepsin	gastric enzyme
ovum	egg cell
platelet	small roundish blood-cell fragment involved in clotting
pineal gland	tiny gland found at the brain's base

peristalsis	wavelike motions in the digestive system that move food
yolk	stored food found in animal eggs
vestigial structure	nonfunctional structure
vitamin	nutrient needed in small quantities for certain bodily functions to properly work
plexus	large cluster of nerves
taxonomy	branch of biology dealing with the classification and naming of living things
stroke	damage to brain cells often caused by lack of circulation
tendon	tissue connecting muscle to bone

PEGGING INFORMATION TO YOUR BODY

Filibustering became a major problem in the Roman Forum, forcing the senators to pass a law prohibiting the use of notes. It was hoped that without notes, senators would be unable to speak for long periods of time. Drawing upon a system developed by the Greeks, senators learned to peg, or mentally link, information to their body parts. This pegging system enabled them to easily memorize huge amounts of information. It is a system that is still popular today.

Research into how the brain stores information indicates that the mind prefers to link new information to older stored memories. There is nothing more familiar to you than your body parts. Wherever you went in life, your body was there too!

Associating new information with specific body parts is the basis for tying a ribbon around your finger to remember something. The glue that sticks new information onto the permanent memory in your brain are strong emotions. These emotions can be funny, painful, or sexual, but they must be exaggerated and extremely intense. Visualizing an extremely emotional link between a part of your body and new information that you need to remember registers this new information in your permanent memory.

Exercise

Learning to memorize information using body-part pegs is easy to learn and a valuable study tool. First, you need to set up a list of body parts that you will use in your associations. These parts will become your hooks, or pegs. Here is a simple list of pegs for you to use:

1. feet		6. stomach	
2. shins		7. heart	
3. knees		8. breasts	
4. thighs		9. shoulders	
5. rear		10. head	

STEP ONE

Take a moment and memorize this peg list. Notice that the parts of the body follow each other in a logical bottom-to-top pattern. This is an aid when trying to remember important information. Stand up while learning this list. Think about and feel the body part, it will help you to remember it.

STEP TWO

Without looking, quickly write down the words on your list. If you have a problem remembering any body part, go back and study the list once again. It is important that you completely remember your list and never forget it.

Using the pegs enables you to link definitions or concepts to these body parts. You accomplish this by visualizing what you study with a body part while imagining some exaggerated action occurring there.

STEP THREE

Here is a list of ten animals that you want to remember for a biology class:

Now imagine a rattler has bitten you on the shin. Feel the fangs penetrating your skin and the pain as the poison slowly floods into your body.

What do you remember when you think of your feet? A canary? Correct. What do you see when you think of your shin? A rattler? Excellent!

Imagine a worm drilling a hole into your knee. It is setting up a nest so it can live inside.

What is biting your shin? Rattler. What is inside your knee? Worm. What is singing on your feet? Canary. Let's continue.

Picture a turtle that has gotten stuck to your rear. Don't ask me how it happened. Maybe you accidentally sat on it. All that matters is that this image is ridiculous and capable of producing strong emotions. Even if it insults, annoys, or disgusts you, these strong emotions will make it easy for you to recall the information.

Quick, what is on your feet? Canary. What is on your knee? Worm. What is stuck to your rear? Turtle. What is biting your shin? Rattler. See how easily you remembered these animals with the pictures your brain formed.

A bear has just ripped open your stomach with its sharp paws and is standing above, preparing to eat you.

Time for another quiz. What is on your shin? Rattler. What is stuck to your rear? Turtle. What is eating your stomach? Bear. Let's continue.

A lion places a paw upon your heart, and it looks as though it might rip your chest wide open if you make the slightest movement.

What is on your rear? Turtle. On your feet? Canary. Shins? Rattler. Knee? Worm. Stomach? Bear. Heart? Lion.

A cat scratches your shoulders so badly the skin is profusely bleeding.

What's on your heart? Lion. Feet? Canary. Knees? Worm. Time for another one.

Imagine swallowing a goldfish, and it is stuck inside your neck. You are choking on the fish.

Quickly, let's remember some animals. Rear? Turtle. Shin? Rattler. Stomach? Bear. Heart? Lion.

Our last animal is a mosquito. Envision millions of mosquitoes crawling over every inch of your exposed head, sucking and biting you. Your flesh agonizes with each new bite.

Time to recall all ten animals:

feet	canary
shins	rattler
knees	worm
rear	turtle
stomach	bear
heart	lion
breasts	dog
shoulders	cat
neck	goldfish
head	mosquitoes

See how easily you remembered all ten animal names. You can expand the number of body parts in your peg list to easily accommodate many more items. Remember to associate vivid, emotionally charged pictures with the body peg to form a permanent memory link.

There is an excellent memory training program called Mega Memory created by Kevin Trudeau that provides even more information on powerful memory-pegging systems. Kevin is a good friend and colleague, and I strongly recommend you invest in this excellent memory program.

USING THE POWER OF MUSIC TO DEVELOP A SUPER MEMORY

A guitar plays two notes and immediately you sing the lyrics of some old Beatles tune from years ago. Lyrics you have never even read. There are thousands of song lyrics in your memory, some going back all the way to your childhood. Yet you can instantly recall lyrics after hearing just a few notes from an instrument.

Psychologists discovered the brain has a natural rhythm that is in harmony with certain types of music. This topic is well described in the book *Super-Learning* by Sheila Ostrander and Lynn Schroeder.

Using music in ¼ or ¾ time with about 60 beats per minute, you can create a tape that enables you to memorize almost anything. These tapes are available from Superlearning Corporation, Suite 500, 450 Seventh Avenue, New York, New York, 10123.

The authors recommend Baroque music that has a natural rhythm of 60 beats per second. One of the finest Baroque composers was Mozart. Some other music recommended by these experts includes:

• Bach—Largo from Harpsichord Concerto in F Minor
• Corelli—Largo from Concerto Number 7 in D Minor, Opus 5

• Vivaldi—Largo from Concerto in D Major for Guitar and Strings

Exercise

To make your own learning tape, first obtain the suggested album. While playing the album on your stereo system, stand in front of the speaker with a small tape recorder. You speak your script directly into the tape recorder; simultaneously, you record the music playing on your stereo system.

Use two four-second intervals when taping your script. During the first four seconds, repeat the concept or definition you want to pair with a stimulus. During the second four seconds, remain silent. Here is a diagram of how to properly make a script:

seconds	seconds
1 2 3 4	1 2 3 4
hola . . . "hello"	silence

Pairing information in this style, and using a four-second interval of silence, you will retain huge amounts of information with very little effort. Your brain believes it is learning the lyrics to a new song and is not aware it is actually learning something significant.

Music's ability to train your mind to recall information is widely known on Madison Avenue. Millions of dollars are spent to create catchy jingles whose lyrics carry the message of a company desiring to sell a product to you. For example, Pepsi Cola hired Ray Charles to sing, "You've got the right one baby." Ray was surrounded by beautiful women, and the company knew that viewers would sit and watch them perform. They didn't want people running to the kitchen during the advertisement. Getting you to sit in front of your screen and listen to him singing guaranteed them that your brain would be conditioned by his message, and that you would learn that Pepsi is the right soda for you to purchase.

If companies can use music to make you learn information that you have no desire to learn, imagine how powerful a tool it will be when you use it to train your brain to retain facts that you need to know.

USING MUSIC TO OVERCOME BOREDOM WHEN STUDYING

While still in college, I learned the value of using music to help me remember technical scientific data. I chose a double major in biology and psychology which required me to take six science courses a semester. Two courses also required attending a lab each week. The formidable amount of information required by these courses combined with my three part-time jobs cut heavily into my free time. On many Saturday nights I studied while my friends were enjoying themselves. Most likely, you too will have days when you have to learn information while those around you pursue more enjoyable experiences.

Having to work when you would rather be having fun with other people can create a negative emotional state, and your mind is less likely to remember facts. Fortunately, there is a way to use music to overcome this dilemma. I discovered this technique one particularly boring Saturday night. I had to memorize biological definitions. One of them was a definition of zoea, which is a crustacean larva. Not very stimulating information to study at 1:00 A.M. on a Saturday night. I started to make up a song that went along to the rhythm of the *West Side Story* song, *Maria*. The song went like this:

> The most beautiful sound I ever heard...
> zoea...zoea...zoea.
> All the most beautiful sounds of the world in a single word. Zoea...zoea...zoea.
> Zoea, I've just seen a thing called zoea.
> Its name almost sounds like diarrhea. Zoea...zoea.

Instead of getting bored while studying biology, I was creating little songs. Suddenly, my work became a creative challenge rather than drudgery. This is an excellent technique for learning large amounts of technical, boring information. Turn your study session into a creativity session by making up songs, poems, and jingles using your key information in their lyrics. Your stimulated mind will actually enjoy learning the information, though the data you must study remains the same. Moreover, the enjoyment you have while learning helps ensure that you will retain the information. As an added bonus, using music to train your memory will also help you remember it faster and recall it more easily.

I studied the definition for zoea in 1968. Ironically, this definition appeared on the examination, and I was one of a very few who knew it. More importantly, after more than 23 years, I can still remember the meaning of the word *zoea*. I remember it because it is musically encoded in my brain. How many of the other students do you think still remember the meaning after more than 23 years? Try this technique for those long, boring study sessions that simply can't be avoided. You won't be disappointed.

CLUSTERING INFORMATION

Your brain prefers clustered information rather than individual units of meaning. Before choosing the number of digits to place in a telephone number, the telephone company spent huge sums of money to determine the ideal number of digits for a telephone number. The company found that the mind works best in units of seven. Actually, a seven-digit telephone number is composed of two numbers. One number is three digits long, while the other is four digits long. Do you notice how annoying it is when someone tells you their telephone number in an unusual sequence? Imagine that someone told you their telephone number was 23755-55, or 23-755-55, or even 2375-5-55. Your brain just doesn't want to remember this information.

Clustering enables your brain to perceive separate units of information as part of a larger single unit. One of the most efficient systems for organizing clustered information is *mnemonics*. Each letter of a word represents a link in a chain that stimulates an association with an important term. For example, when learning the colors of the rainbow, you are taught the mnemonic device ROY G. BIV. The letters in the name ROY G. BIV are the first letters in each of the colors of the rainbow: R = Red, O = Orange, Y = Yellow, G = Green, B = Blue, I = Indigo, and V = Violet. It is much easier to remember the name ROY G. BIV than each individual color.

Many students also learn mnemonic associations in mathematics. The Indian name SOHCAHTOA is a mnemonic device that teaches the fundamental trigonometric relationships. SOH means that the Sine of an angle is equal to the Opposite side divided by the Hypotenuse. CAH means that the Cosine of an angle is equal to the Adjacent side divided by the Hypotenuse. TOA means that the Tangent of an angle is equal to the Opposite side divided by the Adjacent side.

Linking letters to words and phrases is something you should do liberally. The words do not have to mean anything. All they need to do is trigger an association with the basic concepts that each letter represents. While studying biology in college, I created a mnemonic device to memorize the nine characteristics of living things. The nonsense word I created was SMMIGRSAC, a nine-letter word consisting of three syllables that sound like the word SMM-IGR-SAC. Each of these nine letters represents one of nine characteristics of living systems: S = Specific organization, M = Metabolism, M-Movement, I-Irritability, G = Growth, R = Reproduction, S = Specialization, A = Adaption, and C = Control. Instead of spending a tremendous amount of time trying to recall nine separate items, my mind remembered this one word that triggered nine necessary associations.

USING LEARNING SETS

The mind links new information to data already stored in long-term memory. For example, if you read a newspaper article about the president, you add this to the information you already know about him. Your brain functions as if it contained filing folders holding information. When new information is learned, the brain automatically files it in the appropriate folder. Be aware of the types of folders your brain uses to store information. When learning new information, you can consciously link it to the appropriate folder.

Exercise

1. Obtain a copy of the daily newspaper.
2. Read articles about individuals who are well-known to you.
3. Observe how your mind attempts to link the news about these individuals to the information you already possess about them.
4. Develop a habit of reading consciously, always attempting to link new information to data you already know.

USING ENVELOPES TO TEST YOUR MEMORY

An easy way to test your recall of new information is to use an envelope. After studying the meanings of new words and concepts, place the envelope under a line of the text and try to slowly recite what is written on the next line. Move the envelope down and see if you had the right answer. If your answer is correct, continue moving the envelope to the next line. If your answer is incorrect, move the envelope back up a few lines and try again. Continue moving the envelope up and down until you can recall all the lines without error.

MEMORIZING A SCRIPT

At many of my seminars, I meet actors who ask for advice on reading and remembering scripts. Speakers, students, and even salespeople need to remember lengthy presentations using a script similar to one that an actor might use. By using the envelope as described previously, it is easy to learn scripts.

Place the envelope beneath a line of the script. Try to remember the next line without peeking under the envelope. If you correctly identify the next line of the script, continue moving the envelope down. If you make a mistake, continue trying to recall your current line until you get it correct.

Another excellent method for memorizing scripts is to read them aloud and record them on a tape recorder. Place pauses on the tape where your lines should be spoken. Speak the lines of the other characters in the play into your recorder. Leave yourself a long enough pause so that you can recite your lines when the tape is played back during your study session. During your practice, when you hear the lines preceding yours, begin reciting your lines. With practice, you will leave enough blank time on the tape to finish your lines so that you can contrast your recital of them with the lines you have already recorded on the machine. This method will enable you to master even a complicated script quickly. I've used it a number of times with great success.

GETTING YOUR THREE MEMORIES
TO WORK TOGETHER

The brain contains three different memories: short term, intermediate, and long term. The goal of learning is to convert short-term memory into long-term memory. Psychologists believe that short-term memory is an electrical pattern in the brain, one that only briefly exists. For example, if you have an auto accident in which you strike your head, you probably will not remember the accident because the short-term memory is not stored in the long-term memory. The same thing occurs when someone is attacked and struck in the head. After recovery, there is no memory of the attack.

A memory experiment was conducted to measure how long it takes for short-term memory to be converted into long-term memory. Rats were trained to walk a maze shaped like the letter T. After learning the maze, the rats were returned to a cage. The next day, the rats quickly ran to where the food was located. The researchers then began giving shocks to the rats shortly after they had learned the maze. The shocks were designed to short-circuit their short-term memories. The scientists wanted to observe the effects of the shocks on the rats' permanent memories. Rats that were shocked more than an hour after the training session ended displayed no memory loss. Rats shocked less than a few minutes after the training occurred displayed a total memory loss. They required as much time to relearn the maze as it took them to originally learn it. This indicated that it takes about one hour for short-term memory to be converted into long-term memory.

One theory maintains that long-term memory is partly a protein molecule formed in the brain. Another experiment using rats strongly supports this hypothesis. Rats normally prefer the dark. A group of rats was placed in a cage, and every time the room was darkened they were given mild electric shocks. After a short time, the rats became afraid of the dark. The brains of these rats were studied and a new protein called scotophobin (light fear) was found. Amazingly, when normal rats were injected with scotophobin they immediately showed a fear of the dark. Apparently, the fear of the dark was encoded in the scotophobin protein and could be transferred to normal animals by injection.

This experiment has significant implications for many patients who suffer from mental illness, and further research into human applications is now taking place. One day, science may discover the molecular structure of brain memories representing French, calculus, or any other subject. Imagine being given an injection containing the memory proteins for an entire subject! On the negative side, this also could become the ultimate technique for thought control. Who knows what type of messages could be placed into people's minds using these techniques. Perhaps one day, when we develop the wisdom to use this technique, information will be obtained in this fashion instead of through study.

I mentioned that research indicates that it takes about an hour for short-term memory to become permanently converted to long-term memory. Other studies indicate that after studying 50 minutes, you should take a 10- to 15-minute break. This keeps your brain operating at peak efficiency. Failure to take sufficient breaks can result in forgetting much of the information that you believe you learned during studying. It explains why so many students forget information they stayed up all night studying. They did not give their brain sufficient time to store information in its long-term memory. When they tested their retention, they seemed to remember the information before it was in their intermediate memory. Intermediate memory is a temporary memory and does not store itself in long-term memory. As a result, the next day you can forget everything you studied the night before. If you take these recommended breaks, you will actually remember more while working less.

Even if you follow all this advice, studies indicate that 40 percent of all information learned is forgotten within four to six hours after studying when measured by direct recall. Fortunately, there is a way to avoid this problem. Each time you learn the same information, you forget less than you did the last time. Eventually, you do not forget any of the information. It becomes a part of your working knowledge.

There is some information you should never forget. For example, if you go to a hospital and they suspect that you have had a nervous breakdown, they will ask if you remember your name. If you think this is a multiple-choice question, it's a good indication that you've had a breakdown.

REMEMBERING WHAT YOU STUDY

Using the index card system suggested at the start of this chapter is an excellent way to avoid memory loss. Each time you review old index cards, you will be reinforcing the information on them. Eventually, a point is reached where you will never forget what you have learned. By using this technique, you will rediscover anything that you might have forgotten. Then, using this technique, you will easily and quickly form powerful memory traces that will not be forgotten.

When learning on the expertise level, I suggest regularly reviewing all the chapters in a book. Each time you study a new chapter, rapidly scan the old ones you have already completed. Since you've already studied these chapters, taken notes, and used a memory system to retain the information, the data they contain should be well-known to you. Your knowledge of the schema in these books should be extensive, so you will remember what you are reading at very high speed. When linked to your memorization methods, the visual clues and associations gained from constantly reading the chapters will soon make you a master of any information.

A second type of memory is your associative memory. The associative memory is the information you remember when someone asks you a question. The bulk of your memory is in your associative memory.

Your third memory contains information that is difficult for you to recall. It possesses all the information you once knew, but do not remember. This memory is measured by how long it takes for you to relearn information that you once understood. For example, the foreign languages and mathematics studied in high school are often forgotten. If you were going to France and needed to relearn high school French, it would not take you four years to relearn it. It would only take a few weeks. The information may not be retrievable on demand, but with review, it is relearned in a far shorter period of time than it originally took to learn.

To derive the full benefits of this program, I recommend that you practice your high-speed reading exercises in books containing information that you once understood but have forgotten. You will rapidly regain awareness of this information that will then become part of your schema. The more schema you possess, the easier it is to learn new information. This new information also becomes part of your schema. With a rapid gain in your conscious schema, you will experience an exponential growth in your understanding and awareness of life.

Summary

1. You possess an infallible memory. The brain does not forget information, it has difficulty recalling it.

2. Using index cards is an excellent way to memorize vast amounts of information. Any information you do not correctly identify should be written out 25 times and spoken aloud. This will ensure a permanent memory of the information that you can easily recall.

3. Forming associations using powerful emotions helps you remember information more efficiently.

4. You can associate new information with different parts of your body. Use strong imagery and powerful emotions to peg, or attach, the new information to your permanent memory about your body parts.

5. Your brain has a natural rhythm of about 60 beats per second. Using special music, you can instantly memorize up to 200 words per day with almost no effort.

6. Turning boring study sessions into a game that challenges your creativity will make it easier for you to remember information. Try writing songs, poems, and jingles that contain the key facts you need to remember.

7. The brain prefers to learn information that is clustered into a compact grouping rather than individual units. Mnemonic devices are excellent for clustering this type of information.

8. Using an envelope to cover up lines in a book or script is an excellent way to test your recall of the information.

9. The primary goal of study is to convert short-term memory into long-term memory that can easily be recalled.

CHAPTER EIGHT

Mastering Your Mind's Hidden Potential with Meditation

GOALS

- THE OBSTACLES TO MENTAL MASTERY
- DERIVING THE PHYSIOLOGICAL BENE-FITS OF MENTAL FOCUSING
- PREPARING TO FOCUS
- USING COLORS TO ALTER MENTAL STATES
- USING THE RELAXATION RESPONSE TECHNIQUE
- USING PRAYER TO FOCUS THE MIND
- CHOOSING A FOCUSING TECHNIQUE
- OVERCOMING DEPRESSION AND NEGA-TIVE EMOTIONS
- USING THE BRAIN'S CREATIVE POWER

TAPPING YOUR BRAIN'S HIDDEN POTENTIAL

"The mind makes a cruel master, but a wonderful slave," is a popular saying in many cultures. When you think about it, most of life's problems stem from attitudes rather than circumstances. How most people handle a relationship's breakup is a good example. When someone you love says good-bye, your mind keeps returning to this painful experience. Each time you think about the breakup it hurts as if the event had just occurred. You think how nice you were—how dare the other person treat you this way! Where is your pain coming from? Certainly not the other person—it is coming from you. Your mind creates these tormenting thoughts, and is acting as your cruel master. If wrong thinking is the root of many difficulties, then right thinking is the cure.

The reason that thinking is hard to control is because no one teaches you how to control your thoughts. Quite an ironic situation when you think about it. When you purchase a new car, you get a 400-page book describing when to change the oil, rotate the tires, and take care of your engine. When you're born, they give you a smack and wish you the best of luck. No one ever gives you a manual describing how your mind works. You go through life hoping to find clues for developing self-control, but few of us have the good fortune to locate them. Fortunately, some people have found these clues and have developed techniques for mental focusing that can enable you to discipline and control your thoughts.

Focusing the mind is essential for obtaining optimal results from high-speed reading. At my top speed of 1.5

pages per second, even a three-second distraction means missing 4.5 pages. This chapter describes numerous techniques you can immediately use to focus your mind.

DERIVING THE PHYSIOLOGICAL BENEFITS OF MENTAL FOCUSING

Reaching the highest reading speeds imaginable requires a highly disciplined and focused mind. The physiological benefits derived from mental focusing are essential for reaching reading speeds of more than 60 pages per minute. These effects have been closely studied at Harvard Medical School and many other institutions. In fact, many doctors now encourage heart attack victims to learn these stress-reducing techniques.

Doctors use an electroencephalograph, or EEG, to chart the electrical activity of the brain. Mental focusing produces a unique form of consciousness that differs radically from sleep, wakefulness, and even hypnosis. The brain pattern obtained during mental focusing displays numerous, slow alpha waves. These waves correlate with both deep relaxation and creative expression.

Mental focusing causes a drop in blood pressure. Several years ago during a routine office visit to my doctor, I exhibited borderline high blood pressure. I told my doctor I could drop my blood pressure instantly by controlling my bodily functions through mental-focusing techniques. He challenged me to display this ability; within 30 seconds I had dropped my blood pressure 30 points. Lowered blood pressure is a sign of stress reduction and accounts for the wide interest many physicians have in these techniques.

A lowered respiratory rate is also achieved through mental focusing. Slow breathing reduces stress while increasing mental alertness; these two physical benefits can help you accomplish intense mental work at high speed.

Lie detector tests measure the electrical potential of the body, also known as the galvanic skin response. Tension increases this electrical potential, while relaxation lowers it. During mental focusing, the galvanic skin response is dramatically lower, indicating a deep state of rest is being experienced by the subject. Indeed, studies indicate that 20 minutes of mental focusing are equivalent to almost six hours of deep sleep.

Probably one of the greatest physical benefits of mental focusing is its effect upon your blood's chemistry. Your body produces lactic acid, a waste product, as a result of intense muscular activity. Mental focusing lowers the lactic acid level in your blood. Research indicates that lactic acid is directly linked to anxiety attacks, so lowering its level is an important factor in reducing anxiety that can interfere with your high-speed learning.

An experiment testing the effects of lactic acid upon anxiety was performed using two groups of subjects. One group contained anxious subjects, while the other contained ordinary individuals. Each group was given water injections to test their reactions to receiving a shot. None of the ordinary subjects displayed any anxiety, and only a few of the anxious subjects displayed stress. Next, both groups were given a shot containing lactic acid. After the injection, most of the anxious individuals displayed extreme nervousness. Even a few members of the ordinary group developed anxiety symptoms. The experiment clearly indicated that anxiety can be triggered by the level of lactic acid in the blood.

When lactic acid levels rise in a tense individual, the muscles contract and produce even more lactic acid. This cycle continues to build up lactic acid with often catastrophic results. However, mental focusing can reduce tension and lower the lactic acid level. Reduction in lactic acid further reduces tension, producing a cycle of increased relaxation.

Tension and frustration are the adversaries of every super reader. A tired, tense mind cannot function efficiently, and high-speed reading is hampered. Mental focusing helps prevent this problem from even developing.

Your brain is one of the largest consumers of oxygen in your body, relying upon a steady flow of oxygenated blood. Deprived of oxygen for only four minutes, your brain begins to suffer irreparable damage. Mental focusing reduces your body's oxygen consumption rate, allowing more oxygen to reach your brain. During intense studying, your improved use of oxygen enables your mind to learn more rapidly.

Several medical studies indicate that mental focusing over a long period of time can significantly increase both creativity and problem-solving ability. Our society teaches us to accept the limitations of our inherent skills and talents. This often prevents us from trying to master subjects in which we appear to lack talent and ability. Mental focusing develops more than your knowledge, it increases your capacity to learn.

An interesting story concerning this difference between knowledge and understanding was told about Henry Ford. A newspaper reporter wrote a story indicating that Ford was an illiterate because he never completed school. Outraged, Ford sued for slander. During the trial, the reporter asked Ford simple questions any student could easily answer. Ford was unable to answer these questions, so the reporter felt he had proven his case.

Then Ford took the stand. Ford stated he had built a huge library next to his office. Many librarians staffed this library and were on call to research any questions asked by Ford. Ford stated that a wise individual knows where to obtain information, and does not clutter the mind with useless facts. Ford won his case. This case is important to us because it illustrates the importance of knowing how to master information, rather than cluttering your mind with useless details. Mental focusing develops your capacity to understand without relying upon excessive detail.

BECOMING ONE WITH YOUR READING

As the world's fastest reader, I'm often asked what type of books I enjoy reading. I've read hundreds of books on comparative religion, and one of the common factors I've seen in every religion is the reliance upon mental focusing for achieving a heightened state of awareness. Whether you study the religions of the American Indians, or even Christianity, the need to go into a place of deep quiet to achieve a state of concentration is described in the literature.

The feeling of oneness achieved through deep mental focusing helps the super reader become one with the reading material. This is an interesting concept. High-speed reading requires your inner voice to remain silent, but your mind must still absorb the text's information. Initially, you may feel you are not absorbing information. Soon, however, you become aware that your brain is absorbing information even though you cannot "hear it" entering your memory.

One of my students called me a few weeks after attending a seminar. During the workshop, she finished an interesting book in 30 minutes. After going home, she decided she wanted to *really* read the book. To her amazement, when she began reading, she discovered that she already knew all the book's information. She actually learned the material in the book without realizing that the learning was taking place. At first, it is common to feel insecure about retaining textual information. This insecurity stems from your old reading habit that required hearing the words in your mind. Soon, you become accustomed to absorbing information directly into your mind at high speed without the distraction of your inner voice. Confidence will return as you master not only your text, but your mind as well.

Focus your mind before taking important tests, giving a presentation, or obtaining the inner peace necessary for peak performance. Whenever you need to tune out the distractions of everyday life, focus your mind in order to quiet down your inner turmoil. I use this focusing technique before every important television interview. Michael Gelman, the producer of *Live With Regis and Kathy Lee*, invited me to appear on his program. He told me I was going to read a book in a few minutes and then describe its contents—a feat I've successfully accomplished many times. When I arrived, Mr. Gelman told me that the author of the book would also be appearing on the show to test my recall of the material. There is quite a difference between recalling interesting passages of a book and memorizing the same book for an examination. Rather than getting upset, I focused my mind for 90 minutes. Despite the fact that the book was on a topic I knew nothing about, I scored 100 percent on the test questions because my focused mind retained all the important information. You may not need to appear on a national television show, but knowing how to focus your mind will certainly help you perform more efficiently in your life.

Preparing to Focus

There are useful relaxation exercises that will help you concentrate your mind more effectively. These centuries-old breathing exercises are now routinely used by psychologists to help patients quickly reduce stress.

PREPARING TO FOCUS: METHOD ONE

1. Take your right hand and place your thumb on the right nostril.
2. Using your thumb, pinch the right nostril closed.
3. Slowly and gently inhale through your left nostril while counting six seconds.
4. Pinch both nostrils closed and hold for six seconds.
5. Using your ring finger, gently pinch your left nostril closed and exhale for six seconds through your right nostril.
6. Pause for six seconds.
7. Using your ring finger, continue to pinch your left

nostril and inhale for six seconds through your right
nostril.

8. Pinch both nostrils closed, and pause for six seconds.

9. Repeat steps 1 through 8 for five minutes.

Alternating your breathing through each nostril creates
a mild state of euphoria that is quite relaxing. Several
years ago, I wrote a short article on using this technique
to relax in a car during a traffic jam, to relax just before
taking an examination, or even to relax in an office just
prior to an intense meeting. After executing this exercise,
you will be ready to begin your mental focusing technique.

USING COLORS TO ALTER MENTAL STATES

Would you eat a gray hot dog? As disgusting as this
may sound, that is the actual color of the meat before
food coloring is added to it. Without the added red
coloring, few people would eat this food. Psychologists
researching color found it has a powerful effect upon the
mind. Colors can stimulate, relax, anger, or soothe emotions. Food of the wrong color can make us feel sick. An
institution that spends millions to research the psychological effects of color is the Department of Defense. Choosing the proper colors for strategic locations is very
important to them. Submarines, for example, have color
schemes that carefully create the right mood for efficiently
working in very tight quarters for long periods of time.

Colors also can help you focus your mind. Studies
were done on the relationship between seeing and imagining. The brain patterns of individuals were studied
while they focused their eyes upon an apple. Afterward,

they were told to close their eyes and imagine looking at the same apple. The brain patterns of subjects viewing and imagining the apple were identical. Quite simply, it didn't make any difference to their brains if they were seeing or imagining the apple. Perhaps this gives scientific credibility to the biblical concept that "as a man thinks in their mind so shall it be."

Of importance to you is the fact that thinking about colors can replicate the psychological effects of seeing them. To stimulate your mind, visualize the colors red, orange, or yellow. Green and light blue are soothing colors that can relax you.

PREPARING TO FOCUS: METHOD TWO

1. For stimulation of the mind, inhale through both nostrils while imagining the air is colored either red, orange, or yellow.
2. For relaxing the mind, inhale through both nostrils while imagining the air is colored green or light blue.

Body Position for Mental Focusing

The best results from mental focusing occur when you properly position your body. Sit in a chair with your back straight and feet flat on the floor. Place your palms in your lap and gently close your eyes. Most people find that it helps to focus their attention on the area where the mind projects the images of the imagination.

THE RELAXATION RESPONSE TECHNIQUE

Far back in time, our bodies evolved a mechanism that enabled us to fight or flee when confronted by danger.

While this was useful when man was being chased by wild beasts, it often creeps into our modern lives. Many individuals react to the tensions in an office with the same psychological reactions that our ancient ancestors demonstrated when attacked by animals. Unfortunately, these reactions are not quite as useful to us as they were to our ancestors. Research performed at Harvard helped in developing a technique for deep mental focusing. They called this technique *relaxation response* because it triggers the body's natural mechanism for relaxation. The relaxation response technique creates the perfect state for high-speed learning because the deep state of relaxation it creates enables you to focus your mind completely on your text. In this relaxed state, the mind easily absorbs even difficult information.

Using an alarm clock to keep time, this technique should be practiced for a period of 30 minutes each day. The relaxation response is more easily achieved if you use the proper body position described previously. While seated in a chair with your back straight and feet flat on the floor, close your eyes and slowly start to focus upon the number one. Allow no other thoughts to intrude into your stream of awareness. Think to yourself: one . . . one . . . one . . . one. . . . Despite your best efforts, in a short time you probably will experience other thoughts starting to form that interrupt your concentration.

When you are aware that your mind is not focusing upon your number, gently shift your attention to the next digit. If you were thinking of the number one, begin to think of the number two. If you were thinking of the number two, begin to think of the number three, and so on with each successive number.

Avoid becoming distressed or upset by your failure to maintain your concentration. This is quite ordinary and should be expected to occur repeatedly. When first using this method, many find themselves reaching numbers in the hundreds. Slowly but surely, you will find it easier to maintain your concentration upon a specific number.

Exercise

1. Find a comfortable chair and assume the position used for mental focusing.
2. Close your eyes and begin to think of the number one.
3. Focus upon the next number as soon as you are aware that your mind has wandered from your number.
4. Continue this exercise for a total of 30 minutes.

USING PRAYER TO FOCUS THE MIND

Christian monks focused their mind upon a single object, but instead of using a number, they focused upon the object of their devotion. It was common for a monk to sit in a tiny chamber and recite the name Jesus the Christ throughout every waking moment. In one of his books, Mouni Sadhu reports viewing the remains of monks who died centuries ago. Amazingly, their bodies did not decay even with the passage of time. Apparently, spending their entire lives in deep meditation changed the physical properties of their bodies even after death.

The use of prayer to focus the mind can be found in every major religion. Many individuals find reciting a prayer more helpful than simply repeating a number for 30 minutes. If you experience difficulty concentrating upon a single number, consider using a short prayer from your own faith. An excellent prayer for this purpose is the Lord's Prayer.

It is difficult for your mind to wander while focusing on the words of the Lord's Prayer. The prayer is short enough to remember, but long enough to require your total concentration. Other excellent prayers can be found in the book of Psalms. Individuals commonly focused upon the meanings of these prayers to achieve a heightened state of awareness. Almost any inspirational book contains other suitable prayers.

THE LORD'S PRAYER

Our Father who art in heaven, hallowed be Thy name. Thy kingdom come. Thy will be done on earth as it is in heaven. Give us this day our daily bread, and forgive us our debts, as we forgive our debtors. And lead us not into temptation, but deliver us from evil. For Thine is the kingdom, and the power, and the glory, for ever and ever. Amen.

Exercise

1. Sit in your mental focusing position.
2. Set your alarm clock so that it rings after 30 minutes.
3. Begin reciting the Lord's Prayer or one suitable for you.

   Our Father who art in heaven, hallowed be Thy name. Thy kingdom come. Thy will be done on earth as it is in heaven. Give us this day our daily bread, and forgive us our debts, as we forgive our debtors. And lead us not into temptation, but deliver us from evil. For Thine is the kingdom, and the power, and the glory, for ever and ever. Amen.

4. Gently refocus your mind on your prayer if you become distracted.

Concentration

Mouni Sadhu wrote an excellent book on mental concentration that I read many years ago. The book suggests using a watch with a second hand to focus the mind.

Exercise

1. Focus your eyes upon the second hand of the watch.
2. Allow no thoughts to intrude into your mind while focusing your eyes.
3. Attempt to gaze at the watch for a total of five seconds without any intruding thoughts.
4. Each day, add five seconds to the length of time you can focus your mind without interruption.
5. Strive to develop the ability to maintain your mental focusing upon the second hand for a full ten minutes without letting anything distract you.

Choosing a Focusing Technique

Everyone should find a technique that suits their personal tastes. If your mind is very disciplined, you may prefer using a number or focusing upon the second hand of a clock. On the other hand, those with very restless minds may prefer using a prayer. Regardless of the technique you choose, continue to use it regularly to achieve the optimal results.

Focusing Tips

Choosing the proper time to focus can be as important a decision as picking your technique. Find a time when you can consistently perform your focusing exercise. The focusing exercise works best when it is repeated at the same time each day. Do not eat before mental focusing. Eating diverts blood to your stomach and intestines and away from your brain.

Twenty minutes of mental focusing is the equivalent of six hours of sleep. Some people find it difficult to sleep if they practice focusing late in the evening, while others experience the opposite effect. I am one of those who finds that focusing late at night helps me to release the tensions of the day, making sleep easy to achieve. Daily use of mental focusing is the single most helpful thing you can do to help draw upon your brain's full power.

Overcoming Depression and Negative Emotions

You often hear we are in the age of depression. Depression and other negative emotions drain you of the vitality necessary for intense mental work. Successful studying and recalling are difficult when your emotions are draining your energy. Fortunately, there are simple techniques that you can use to overcome some of these problems.

Music can help you overcome the draining effects of many negative emotions. Ideally, your music should contain no lyrics and should remind you of positive experiences from a more joyful period in your life. Many of the lullabies you enjoyed during childhood are perfect choices.

Your brain works like a cheap calculator that has only one memory. It only focuses efficiently upon one thing at a time. Negative feelings cease to exist when you stop concentrating upon them. Instead of spotlighting your negative emotions, play the soothing music repeatedly in your mind. Soon the negative feelings will dissipate due to a lack of attention.

Eliminating Anxiety

Unlike depression, anxiety usually consists of concerned thoughts about a future event. Dispelling anxiety is best accomplished by focusing upon a prayer. Instead of focusing upon a disturbing thought, your mind focuses upon a positive thought that is the complete opposite of whatever is troubling you. For example, if you are anxious about taking a test, think about how successful you will be. Energy follows thought, and as you think, so it shall be.

Once again, the Lord's Prayer is ideally suited for dispelling anxiety. When you are anxious, repeating it throughout the day helps to seed the mind with positive thoughts. Another excellent prayer for liberation from inner troubles is the prayer of Saint Ephraem the Syrian.

O lord and dispenser of my life,
save me from the spirit of frustration, dejection,
lust, and prating.

But Grant to me, thy servant, the spirit of purity,
humility in wisdom, patience and love.
O my lord and master! Enable me to see my own
iniquities and not to judge my brother!
For blessed art thou forever. Amen.

Although an excellent prayer, it is a bit long for some
people to remember, especially while anxious. An easier
prayer to remember under extreme stress is: "Thou will
keep them in perfect peace whose mind is stayed on
thee." Though short, the prayer has the power to focus
the mind under the worst conditions. In 1985, my mother
was dying from pancreatic cancer; I taught her to use this
prayer to overcome the pain. It helped her overcome
some of the most severe suffering I ever saw anyone
endure. I'm sure it will help you overcome the type of
anxiety that occurs in everyday life.

Never accept negative emotions or thoughts as a necessary part of life. The world is full of joy, all the pain
exists within us. We have the power to create within
ourselves whatever type of rhythm we choose in our
lives. Choosing properly helps ensure success in all your
endeavors. Achieving the highest levels of super reading
requires regular use of these techniques.

USING THE BRAIN'S CREATIVE POWER

The more information stored in your brain, the greater
your creative potential. Your brain has the ability to
integrate stored information with other information to
create new ideas and concepts. Some of the most important breakthroughs occurred when individuals integrated

information obtained from their hobbies into their professions.

A good example of this happened earlier in this century. Physicists trying to identify the structure of the atom were having difficulty determining the positions of the electrons. Were the electrons located in specific places, or were they floating around loosely like grapes in a pudding? Bohr uncovered this mystery by using information he obtained from his hobby as a musician.

Bohr discovered that the position of electrons followed the same mathematical formula as that which determined the position of notes on a violin string. Since Bohr played the violin, it was easy for him to see this relationship; it was one that revolutionized our understanding of the universe.

By using your super-reading skills, you will also be able to tap your full creative power. As you increase your reading, your schema will also increase. This will enable you to see things by using perspectives unavailable to you in the past. Imagine several people observing the sunset. One is an astronomer and observes the earth rotating away from the sun's light. The second individual is an artist who sees the beautiful colors of the sunset as the inspiration for a painting. The third is a police officer who recognizes that the crime rate is about to rise as day changes into night. After reading books about astronomy, art, and crime, you will see the sunset from the viewpoints of the astronomer, artist, and police officer. You will begin to live life more multidimensionally, which ultimately will help you become all you are capable of becoming.

Summary

1. Mental focusing lowers the galvanic skin response; changes the brain-wave pattern; reduces the blood pressure; lowers the respiratory rate; lowers the blood's lactic-acid level; and reduces oxygen consumption.

2. Alternating your breathing through each nostril can produce an instant state of relaxation.

3. Focusing on colors can increase or decrease your stress and alertness levels.

4. Using numbers as a mental focal point produces a highly focused mind that easily learns and retains information at high reading speeds.

5. Traditional prayers also can be used to concentrate thought while eliminating distressing emotions.

6. Fixing the eyes upon the second hand of a watch is a useful technique for perfecting mental concentration.

7. Calming music can help you overcome feelings of depression that interfere with learning.

8. Prayer and mental-focusing techniques enable you to overcome anxiety.

9. Regular use of these techniques increases your super-reading productivity.

10. Your ability to read more will not only increase your schema, but also will provide you with an ability to view events more multidimensionally.

CHAPTER NINE

How to Integrate Your Super-Reading Skills

GOALS

- INTEGRATING YOUR SUPER-READING
  SKILLS
- TESTING YOUR SUPER-READING SKILLS
- SCORING HIGH ON EXAMS
- USING SUPER READING FOR OTHER
  PURPOSES

It's time to put your super-reading skills to the test
by using the several sample reading units contained in
this chapter. I will guide you through all the steps
necessary for reading, studying, and using this information to pass the sample examinations found at the
end of each unit. Useful tips for scoring high on exams
are also offered. You will be amazed at how easily you
can learn the information necessary for passing these
sample tests.

STEP ONE
PREPARING TO FOCUS THE MIND

Before you read these sample units, you must put your mind into a receptive learning state. Use the deep-breathing exercise described in Chapter Eight prior to performing your mental-focusing technique.

Sitting comfortably, pinch your right nostril closed and slowly inhale to a count of six through your left nostril. Hold your breath for a count of six. Now pinch your left nostril closed and exhale to a count of six through your right nostril. Hold your breath to a count of six, and still pinching your left nostril, inhale through your right nostril to a count of six. Again, hold your breath to a count of six, pinch your right nostril closed, and exhale through your left nostril. Pause to a count of six, and continue this entire cycle for a total of five minutes. Remember, you are continually alternating the side of your nose through which you inhale and exhale. Inhale on one side of your nose and exhale on the other for a count of six while pausing to a count of six between inhalation and exhalation. Begin your breathing exercise now, and return to this book when you are finished.

STEP TWO
FOCUSING YOUR MIND

Focusing your mind will help you more efficiently study the material contained in these sample units. Use the relaxation-response technique described in Chapter Eight.

Set an alarm clock so that it awakens you after 20

minutes. Sit in a chair with your back straight and feet flat on the floor. Close your eyes and slowly begin to repeat the number one. Hear your inner voice repeat this number very gently, "one, one, one...." When your mind becomes distracted, gently begin focusing upon the number two. Each time your mind is distracted, continue to focus upon the next whole number. Stop when your alarm clock rings. Begin your mental focusing now, and return to this book when you are done.

STEP THREE
PRACTICING READING AT THE STUDY LEVEL

You are about to study the sample units contained in this chapter. You will want to use the suggestions on studying technical material that are contained in Chapter Six. When you finish studying each unit, you can take a short test to determine how well you have learned the material.

To help you study more efficiently, the key concepts and definitions that you need to remember in the first unit will be in boldface type.

Testing Your Super-Reading Skills

REVIEW OF STEPS FOR MASTERING DIFFICULT MATERIAL

1. Before studying the information in any specific unit, skim all the sample units at your top speed. Pay close attention to the principal concepts and your familiarity

with the material. Observe if any information begun in one unit is continued in another unit.

2. After skimming all the units, begin to study each unit one at a time. Begin studying each specific unit by skimming its contents to analyze how far you can read before forgetting information. Break down the unit into small, easy-to-remember sections.

3. Begin reading the first section at your top speed. Pay attention to the primary ideas and principles contained within this section. Place small marks in the margin to indicate the concepts and definitions you expect to see on the sample examination following the unit.

4. Read the first section at your comprehension speed, marking off additional concepts and definitions that you suspect will appear on the sample examination.

5. Study the marked-off section by using index cards, as suggested in Chapter Seven.

6. Begin studying the next section of the unit following steps 2 through 5.

SAMPLE UNIT ONE

Earlier in this century physicists knew that the **atom contained negatively charged particles, called electrons, spinning around a nucleus,** but they were not certain of the electrons' location. Some believed that electrons looked like grapes in a pudding. This model pictured **electrons randomly positioned** in the atom. Other scientists believed that the **electrons held distinct locations** within the atom. The **answer** to this mystery would be **discovered by Bohr,** one of the early pioneers in quantum theory. Bohr's research revolutionized our perception of reality, and science has never been the same.

Bohr suspected the electrons occupied specific positions rather than random ones. His painstaking investigation confirmed his hypothesis, but to his amazement, the positions held by electrons **followed a pattern** he had seen before while studying **music.**

Look at the frets on a guitar or any other stringed instrument. Notice that the **distances between each fret are not equal; instead, the farther down the string you go, the closer together the notes become.** It is possible to **describe the distances separating these notes with equations. These equations** also **describe** the relative positions of the electron orbits. **Actually, the first individual to notice this special interval was the famous mathematician Pythagoras.** On the atomic level, the structure of matter appears to follow the same mathematical laws as music! Even more amazing is that with **the exception of Uranus, Neptune, and Pluto, the positions held by the planets in our solar system also follow the Pythagorean interval.**

Bohr's discovery upset the very foundations of physics. Since **Newton's time, it was believed that the universe followed a very continuous pattern. Bohr's universe was discontinuous. Electrons could not randomly exist in an atom, but only at very specific levels called quanta.**

The **quantum pattern** is quite similar to the arrangement of **seats in a typical auditorium.** In an auditorium, you can choose to **sit in any seat** you desire, but **not in the spaces separating the rows of seats. In a** continuous situation, there would be no seats, and you could choose to sit at any position in the room.

More recently, a radical **new theory** has evolved in quantum physics that states that the **universe is built upon extremely tiny points of vibration called strings.** String theory attempts to explain all the physical laws by the relative vibrations of these extremely tiny points. The string theory also implies that the universe is patterned upon many of the principles found in music.

Interestingly, **every major religion contains information indicating that our universe is following a musical pattern.** For example, in the **Jewish and Christian faiths, God is often pictured in the center of singing angels. In the East, the deity is often pictured as either singing or dancing to the creation of the universe.** It is known that the **Psalms** found in the Old Testament once **were played to music** that was lost many centuries ago. Those who investigate the history of religion believe that **music made the Psalms even more powerful.** Can it be that the **ancient seekers of truth were describing in their parables the same truths that scientists are beginning to observe with their instruments?** Is the main difference between these systems the type of language used to describe the phenomena? Many physicists believe this is the case.

STEP FOUR
PREPARING INDEX CARDS FOR STUDYING SAMPLE UNIT ONE

I've prepared a listing of the information to be placed on your index cards for studying Sample Unit One. It indicates which information should be written on the front and on the back of your cards. Obtain a package of 3″ × 5″ index cards, and copy this information onto them.

CARD 1

Front: What are electrons?

Back: Negatively charged particles spinning around a nucleus

CARD 2

Front: What two models of electron positions originally existed?

Back: Random or specific location

CARD 3

Front: Who discovered the position of electrons?

Back: Bohr

CARD 4

Front: What did Bohr originally believe about the pattern of electrons?

Back: Bohr suspected electrons followed a specific pattern

CARD 5

Front: What did Bohr's electron pattern appear to be following?

Back: The pattern of musical notes on a fretted instrument

CARD 6

Front: Who originally discovered the special interval that Bohr found existed in atoms?

Back: Pythagoras

CARD 7

Front: Which planets do not follow the special interval?
Back: Uranus, Neptune, and Pluto

CARD 8

Front: What pattern do most planets in our solar system
obey?
Back: The Pythagorean interval

CARD 9

Front: How did Newton's universe appear to be organized?
Back: Continuously

CARD 10

Front: How did Bohr's universe appear to be organized?
Back: Discontinuously

CARD 11

Front: What is the name given to the specific electron
levels?
Back: Quanta

CARD 12

Front: What does the quantum pattern look like?
Back: Like the specific positions of seats in a typical
auditorium

CARD 13

Front: What is string theory?
Back: Theory stating the universe is built upon tiny
vibrating points

CARD 14

Front: What does the string theory indicate?

Back: Universe is built upon musical principles

CARD 15

Front: What principle of the creation does every major religion have in common?

Back: Principle of music

CARD 16

Front: How is God described in the Jewish and Christian faiths?

Back: Surrounded by singing angels

CARD 17

Front: How is the deity described in Eastern religions?

Back: Either singing or dancing to the creation of the universe

CARD 18

Front: How were the Psalms originally used?

Back: Were played to music

CARD 19

Front: What effect did music have upon the Psalms according to many researchers?

Back: Increased their power

CARD 20

Front: What is the relationship between the ancient models of creation and modern ones?

Back: Both indicate the universe is built upon musical principles

Take the index cards you have just created and shuffle them into a random order. Look at the front side of an index card, then recite aloud the information you believe is contained on the back side. If you answer correctly, place the index card in the first pile. If you answer incorrectly, write the correct answer 25 times while saying it aloud. Place the index cards you incorrectly answered on the second pile. When you complete the first pile, take the second pile containing the index cards you incorrectly identified and reshuffle it. Repeat these steps until you correctly identify all the information on the index cards.

Tips for Scoring High on Exams

Just as super-reading skills can help you rocket through text, they also can help you score high on examinations. Before taking any examination, practice your mental-focusing techniques. This not only concentrates your mind on the exam, it helps you avoid becoming anxious or depressed.

The various types of questions found on tests require using different portions of your memory. It is not necessary for you to recall each specific answer on multiple-choice questions. Multiple-choice questions only require you to recognize the correct answer using your associative memory. The associative memory contains most of the information stored in memory, and it is the easiest memory to use when needing to answer a question.

Fill-in-the-blank questions require direct recall of literal information and are therefore more difficult to answer. Using index cards, pegging, and the other suggestions contained in Chapter Seven will help you recall this information when needed.

Essay questions typically are the most difficult items on tests. They require an extensive use of direct recall for correct answers. If you followed my suggestion and stored information using all your senses and visualization skills, you will be able to recall most of the information by re-creating the images and feelings associated with the data.

Most tests contain schematic information you can use to answer questions. For example, the choices found in a multiple-choice question often provide information you can use for answering an essay or fill-in-the-blank questions elsewhere in the test. Since certain questions often contain useful information for answering other questions, it is important to skim every examination quickly before answering any questions. During your skimming, analyze the types of questions contained on the examination to determine how difficult they will be to answer. Plan your time appropriately. If you find easy sections, complete them quickly so you can spend more of your time answering the difficult test questions. Do not spend more than two to five minutes analyzing the test.

Taking Standardized Tests

You probably will take some standardized tests during your lifetime. These tests usually present an essay, followed by questions about the essay's content. Always read the questions before reading the essay. Use your visualization skills to create a picture about the question being asked. While reading the essay you will recognize the portion of text containing the answer to the question. Using this technique, I scored an 800 on the Biology Graduate Record Examination—a score in the 99th percentile. Not bad for a student who got *C* grades in biology till his senior year of college, the year I finally learned how to use these skills. You will obtain similar results.

UNIT ONE SAMPLE EXAMINATION

(ANSWERS CONTAINED IN APPENDIX ONE) READ THE FOLLOWING QUESTIONS AND PLACE THE CORRECT ANSWER IN THE BLANK SPACE PROVIDED.

1. ＿＿ Choose the answer that best describes electrons: (a) positively charged particles (b) neutral particles (c) negatively charged particles (d) none of these answers

2. ＿＿ Who discovered the electron's position in the atom? (a) Newton (b) Bohr (c) Einstein (d) none of these answers

3. ＿＿ Which planets do not follow the Pythagorean interval? (a) Sun, Moon, Earth (b) Mercury, Mars, Jupiter (c) Venus, Jupiter, Saturn (d) Uranus, Neptune, Pluto

4. ＿＿ Newton's universe appeared to be organized: (a) continuously (b) discontinuously (c) straight (d) none of these answers

5. ＿＿ Bohr's universe appeared to be organized: (a) continuously (b) discontinuously (c) straight (d) none of these answers

6. ＿＿ Which of the following most closely resembles Bohr's quantum model? (a) people

sitting on auditorium seats (b) people sitting on a beach (c) people sitting on the grass at a concert (d) people standing in a movie line

7. ____ What principle of the creation does every major religion have in common? (a) kosher food (b) reincarnation (c) principle of music (d) none of these answers

8. ____ How were the Psalms originally used? (a) played to music (b) used the same as today (c) used silently (d) none of these answers

9. ____ Who originally discovered the special interval that Bohr found in atoms? (a) Plato (b) Aristotle (c) Pythagoras (d) Newton

10. ____ What did Bohr's electron pattern seem to follow? (a) the pattern of the sunset (b) no pattern (c) the pattern of musical notes on a fretted instrument (d) Newton's pattern

READ EACH OF THE FOLLOWING QUESTIONS AND PLACE YOUR BEST ANSWER IN THE BLANK SPACE PROVIDED.

11. The Psalms were originally used with ____.

12. ____ discovered the positions of electrons in atoms.

13. Newton's universe appeared to be ____.

14. ____ is the special name given to the positions electrons have in an atom.

15. Name the three planets not following the Pythagorean interval: ____, ____, and ____.

16. The theory that the universe is built upon tiny vibrating points is called the ____ theory.

17. In the Jewish and Christian faiths, God is often pictured as being surrounded by ____ ____.

18. The tiny negatively charged particles circling the nucleus of an atom are called ____.

19. _____ is the famous physicist whose model of the universe was continuous.
20. The quantum pattern looks like _____ _____.

Notice how many of the answers to the fill-in-the-blank questions can be answered using information found in the multiple-choice questions. On most tests you probably will not find this many questions capable of being answered using information from other questions, but you will find a large amount of useful information that can help you score higher on exams while working faster.

SAMPLE UNIT TWO
MORE OF THE AMAZING PARADOX OF LIGHT

The simple act of gazing at the light of a distant star creates a fascinating paradox. Traveling the huge distance separating a star from the earth often requires the light to take hundreds of thousands of earth years to reach us. While this is the amount of time that passes for an observer on earth, the particles of light that are making the trip arrive on earth at the exact same time as they left the star! How can that be?

Researchers in quantum physics have evidence supporting the theory that time is a relative concept. The faster you move, the slower time becomes. They tested this theory using atomic clocks, the most accurate time-measuring devices that exist. Two atomic clocks having identical times were used. One clock was launched in a space ship at the highest speeds we are now capable of achieving. When the clock returned to earth, the space-born clock's time differed significantly from the time shown by its earthbound twin. Apparently, traveling at high speed slowed down time enough to affect the clock.

Scientists believe that at the speed of light there is no time. The waves of light traveling from distant stars to earth are moving at 186,000 miles per second. This means these rapidly moving particles exist outside of time, and arrive on our planet at the same time that they left the distant star. As an observer, you are not moving at the speed of light, and exist in a different time reality than the time frame of the photon. Although no time has passed for this tiny particle, hundreds of thousands of years have passed for you. Though hard to imagine, these particles actually occupy both places at the same time. This appears to be true according to modern quantum theory.

Even more amazing is the belief that your observation of a star's light actually changes its physical properties. Traveling through the vacuum of space, light appears to be a wave. When seen by your eye, the light takes on the properties of a particle. Waves and particles are complete opposites in physics. Waves have no weight and occupy no specific location, while particles have specific weight and occupy a specific place. Your simple observation of a star's light wave converts it from a wave into a particle. The fact that your consciousness can alter the physical properties of light is another of quantum theory's dramatic paradoxes (paradoxes that are supported by experimental evidence).

THE SHOCKING PARADOX OF ELECTRICITY

Electricity moves at the same speed as light, 186,000 miles per second. Physicists suspected that a particle of light was contained within the flow of electricity. Somehow this particle was accelerating the electricity to the speed of light. Yet, close observation of electricity indicated that no photon could be found. Finally, quantum physicists developed the theory that two different types of light particles exist. The first particle, called the photon, is real. It is the particle of light that you see when looking at a light. A ghost particle of light, called a virtual photon, is also believed to exist. Virtual photons exist for an infinitesimally short span of time. Indeed, they exist so briefly that they do not seem to actually exist, but only appear along enough to affect the rate of motion of electrical particles. Scientists believe that these ghost particles materialize for an instant, push the electrons to the speed of light, then instantly disappear without leaving a trace. Virtual photons literally exist and don't exist at the same time!

NOW YOU SEE IT—NOW YOU DON'T

Virtual photons are not the only particles that seem to disappear and then reappear. The single electron found in a hydrogen atom also displays this curious property. Scientists developed a technique for photographing the position of the electron in a hydrogen atom. They took a series of photographs and found that the electron occupied one of two places on opposite sides of the atom's nucleus, or center. No matter how many or how quickly pictures were taken, the electron was always seen in one of the two positions. It was never observed moving from one position to the other. Scientists were puzzled.

This incredible phenomenon is easier to understand if you imagine for a moment three chairs arranged in a row. Your friend sits on the chair on the right and you take his picture. You walk out of the room and when you return, you find your friend sitting in the chair on the left. Again you take his picture and leave the room. Upon returning, you see that your friend is once again sitting on the chair on the right. You decide you want to get a picture of your friend traveling from one chair to the other. So you try to trick your friend by leaving the room and returning very quickly. No matter how often or how quickly you return to the room, your friend manages to switch chairs without you seeing your friend move. How can this be?

The solution to this mystery won the Nobel prize for a physicist named Bell. Bell theorized that while traveling, the electron disappeared from our universe. It actually entered into a different reality that exists beyond our time and space. In that other reality, the particle moved to the other position, and then instantly appeared in its new position in our universe.

Although this may seem impossible, Dr. Thomas Bearden, one of our nation's top military physicists, believes it is true. Bearden's work is of great interest to Strategic Defense, an important agency in the U.S. Defense Department. I met him while lecturing in Huntsville, Alabama. Bearden believes that new psychotronic weapons have been developed in Russia and can project nuclear warheads through the same altered dimension that electrons travel. He describes a technology that in theory enables a warhead to be exploded over Russia and then instantly projected over Washington without using a missile. While in Huntsville, I found other scientists who took Bearden's model very seriously.

After reading this unit, place the important concepts and definitions that you found on index cards. After completing your study, take the Unit Two Sample Examination.

UNIT TWO SAMPLE EXAMINATION

(ANSWERS CONTAINED IN APPENDIX ONE)
READ THE FOLLOWING QUESTIONS AND PLACE THE CORRECT ANSWER IN THE BLANK SPACE PROVIDED.

1. _____ To an observer on earth, the light traveling from distant stars: (a) arrives instantly (b) takes considerable time (c) both of these answers (d) neither of these answers

2. _____ To the photon of light traveling to earth from a distant star, the time it takes to make the trip is: (a) instantaneous (b) very long (c) both of these answers (d) neither of these answers

3. _____ What effect does speed have upon time? (a) no effect (b) slows time at high speeds (c) time goes faster at high speeds (d) there is no effect

4. ____ Scientists researched the effect of speed on time by using: (a) atomic clocks (b) hour glasses (c) sun dials (d) wristwatches

5. ____ Your observation of star light can: (a) have no effect on it (b) change it from a wave to a particle (c) change it into sound (d) none of these answers

6. ____ Characteristics of waves include: (a) weight and definite location (b) no weight and no location (c) both of these answers (d) neither of these answers

7. ____ Characteristics of particles include: (a) weight and definite location (b) no weight and no location (c) both of these answers (d) neither of these answers

8. ____ The speed of electricity is: (a) 1,000 miles per hour (b) 10,000 miles per second (c) 100,000 miles per hour (d) 186,000 miles per second

9. ____ Virtual photons are (a) real particles that exist for long periods of time (b) imaginary particles that do not exist at all (c) particles that exist for extremely short periods of time (d) none of these answers

10. ____ The electron in a hydrogen atom appears to: (a) disappear and reappear in a new place (b) stay in the same place (c) move slowly (d) change into a virtual photon

READ EACH OF THE FOLLOWING QUESTIONS AND PLACE YOUR BEST ANSWER IN THE BLANK SPACE PROVIDED.

11. The invisible particle of light that physicists believe exists in electricity is called a ____ ____.

12. As an object speeds up, time ____ down.

13. Studies on the effects of speed on time use very accurate ____ clocks.

14. Something lacking mass and location could be a ____.

15. Something possessing mass and location could be a ____.

16. Dr. Bearden believes that the Russians have developed ____ weapons that can project nuclear warheads through another dimension.

17. The physicist who won the Nobel prize for explaining the movement of the hydrogen electron is Dr. ____.

18. When you observe starlight, your observation ____ its properties from a wave to a particle.

19. The speed of light is ____ miles per second.

20. Bearden's work is of great interest to ____ ____, an important agency in the U.S. Defense Department.

SAMPLE UNIT THREE
SUPER CONDUCTIVITY

Over the last few decades, chronic shortages of energy have plagued our nation and devastated our environment. Dr. Bearden told me about a fantastic breakthrough made in Alabama that will help solve this problem.

Energy demands are highest during the day, and much lower at night. Power plants have the capacity to generate more power during the evening, but no way to store the electricity economically for use during the day. Bearden told me about a breakthrough made in super conductivity that may eliminate this problem.

When electricity travels through wires, some of the power is lost as heat. Touch a wire that is connected to a machine that has been running for many hours and you probably can feel the heat of the wire. Super conductivity permits electricity to flow through a wire without any friction so that there is virtually no loss of power. Unfortunately, conventional super conductivity requires using special substances at extremely low temperatures that are prohibitively expensive to produce on a large scale. Recently, a technique for producing super conductivity at relatively hot temperatures was developed in Alabama. This technique may make it economical to store large amounts of power in super-cooled coils.

Imagine a coil of super-cooled wire in a structure the size of a baseball park. During the evening, the electricity would be shunted into this coil. The power would spin around this frictionless wire throughout the night and be ready for use in the morning. The super-cooled coil would act as a gigantic low-cost battery, enabling utilities to produce power more efficiently. More importantly, it would also permit more widespread use of other types of power that are currently impractical. The power of the tides has long been viewed by scientists as a source of energy. However, the tides only last for a brief amount of time, and the power generated by them can not be stored for later use. Using super-cooled coils, it may be possible to make use of this power source as well as solar power. Energy generated by the sun during the day could finally be stored and used during the evening by using super-cooled coils.

These super-cooled coils already are being put to use in advanced computer systems. The lack of friction that occurs in these wires enables computers to operate at incredibly high speeds.

CHANGING ENERGY INTO MATTER

Perhaps the most amazing breakthrough that Bearden shared with me was the discovery of how to change energy into matter. Einstein's equation $E = MC^2$ says that energy is matter moving very quickly. Yet the opposite is also true: matter is energy moving very slowly. Bearden described a method for infinitely slowing down a flow of electricity so it can be turned into matter.

To freeze energy into matter you need to start with an electron beam—an easy thing to obtain. You probably have several of them in your house. Fluorescent lamps and television tubes both use electron beams to create light.

Imagine a fluorescent lamp stripped of its outside so that only the inner electron beam is present. If you placed a wave generator on all four sides of this beam you could create a very interesting phenomenon. Remember in high school how a plus one and minus one equaled zero? If our wave generators are creating waves that are the exact opposite of each other, then they should cancel each other out and equal zero as shown in the picture. What would happen if the place where the waves cancel each other wasn't empty? Suppose the electron beam was at the position where this cancellation takes place. You would have the infinite pressure of the waves canceling each other to equal zero pushing against the electron flow. Electrons are so tiny you can't compress them. In effect, what you have created is an infinite pressure upon an immovable object. According to Bearden, the electricity freezes into a new form of energy he calls a scalar wave.

Physicists know the energy wave patterns of many forms of matter. You could use any of these patterns to form a scalar wave. For example, if you used the wave pattern of tin in two of the generators, and the opposite pattern opposed them, you would freeze the electrical flow using a tin-wave pattern. Bearden claims that if you create a second scalar wave by using the exact same wave pattern, and then cross both these two scalar beams at right angles, the energy changes into physical matter. Bearden has written about this fascinating subject in his book, *Excalibur Briefing*. The book even contains the patent number on the scalar generator with instructions on how it works.

Dr. Bearden told me that many years ago, the scientific genius, Nikola Tesla, discovered these principles. Bearden has built a working scalar generator that I have not seen. However, other scientists I spoke with in Huntsville confirmed that the device does exist and can create various types of matter from energy. Bearden believes the universe is constructed from the solidification of scalar waves.

BACK TO THE FUTURE—FOR REAL

Bearden told me about experiments that have been successfully performed on time travel. Quarks are the tiny building blocks that form protons, neutrons, and electrons, the components of the atom. In the time-reversal experiment, quarks are sent into the past. The experiment is designed to reverse the flow of quarks from the present into the past. Just before the experiment begins, the local concentration of quarks increases to a significant level, indicating that the experiment affects the past environment.

CURING THE INCURABLE

Bearden published an article describing how a wave device was constructed by a French physician named Antoine Priore. Priore took electronic pictures of tumors that were turning into cancers, and played back the wave patterns in reverse by using a wave generator. His research indicated that the cancerous tumors responded to these reverse wave patterns by returning to normal tissue, like a movie being played in reverse on a VCR. Dr. Bearden believes that since the universe is built from energy patterns, even living tissue can be affected when subjected to the proper type of energy waves.

CONCLUSION

While this work is still controversial and not widely accepted in traditional circles, my discussions with Dr. Bearden and other scientists indicate there is more truth to these claims than most people would care to believe. If these ideas are eventually proven to be true, it will open a new era for all of mankind. Imagine being able to create water in barren deserts using scalar-wave generators, or curing diseases by reversing the energy patterns of the disease using time-reversed scalar waves. Whether truth or fiction, Bearden's ideas are both fascinating and inspiring. I wait with great anticipation for future reports from this interesting scientist.

UNIT THREE SAMPLE EXAMINATION
(ANSWERS CONTAINED IN APPENDIX ONE)

READ THE FOLLOWING QUESTIONS AND PLACE THE CORRECT ANSWER IN THE BLANK SPACE PROVIDED.

1. _____ Energy demands are highest: (a) in the evening (b) on weekends (c) during the day (d) none of these answers

2. _____ When energy travels through wires, some of the power is lost as: (a) taxes (b) light (c) time (d) heat

3. _____ Super conductivity permits electricity to flow through a wire without any: (a) cost (b) light (c) friction (d) special conditions

4. _____ Conventional super conductivity requires: (a) very low temperatures (b) lots of time (c) batteries (d) high temperatures

5. _____ A super-conductivity coil could store electricity just like a: (a) battery (b) boiler room (c) traditional electric plant (d) nuclear reactor

6. _____ The new super conductors could make what type of energy more efficient: (a) tidal power (b) solar power (c) both of these answers (d) neither of these answers

7. ___ A scalar wave is a form of frozen: (a) water (b) light (c) electricity (d) matter

8. ___ The types of particles sent back through time in Bearden's experiment were: (a) electrons (b) neutrons (c) protons (d) quarks

9. ___ The French physician who cured cancer using time-reversed scalar waves is: (a) Priore (b) Pierre Le Font (c) Alec Pryer (d) none of these answers

10. ___ Bearden's ideas are: (a) widely accepted (b) highly controversial (c) completely false (d) completely proven

READ EACH OF THE FOLLOWING QUESTIONS AND PLACE YOUR BEST ANSWER IN THE BLANK SPACE PROVIDED.

11. The method for producing frictionless electricity is called ___ conductivity.

12. Bearden calls waves of frozen electricity ___ waves.

13. The formula that demonstrates that energy and matter are related was discovered by ___.

14. The principles behind scalar-wave production were first discovered by the scientific genius ___.

15. The French physician who used time-reversed waves to cure cancer was ___.

16. The tiny subparticles that were sent back through time were called ___.

17. According to Dr. Bearden, you need ___ scalar waves to create matter from energy.

18. ___ and ___ are two common objects found in the home that contain electron generators.

19. Super conductors could be used to store ___.

20. Most scientists consider Dr. Bearden's ideas ___.

OTHER PURPOSES FOR SUPER READING

Congratulations! You now possess the super-reading skills necessary to become all you are capable of becoming. The challenges of life are best tackled using the solutions developed by the world's wisest men and preserved in books. Use your new learning skills to learn the secrets you could never find the time to learn before.

Our world faces more challenges to its survival today than perhaps at any other time in its history. I believe that as we develop the ability to master our own problems, we are helping to reduce the overall burden of the planet. Many of us often pray to God for help in times of crisis. I'd like to think that those who possess super-reading skills will act differently. Instead of asking for God's help, they will ask, "How can I help?" I wish you the best of success. Using the skills you now possess, I know you can obtain it.

Summary

1. When taking a test, always completely read it before answering any questions.
2. Look for information contained in exam questions that you can use to answer other questions on the test.
3. Always read the questions on standardized tests before reading the essays.

BIBLIOGRAPHY

Edwin S. Babbitt, *The Principles Of Light And Color. The Healing Power Of Color*, University Books, 1967.

Thomas E. Bearden, *Excalibur Briefing: Explain Paranormal Phenomena*, Strawbery Hill Press, A Walnut Hill Book, 1988.

Robert F. Biehler and Jack Snowman, *Psychology Applied to Teaching*, Houghton Mifflin Company, 1986.

Judson Seise Brown, *The Motivation Of Behavior*, McGraw-Hill, 1961.

William G. Browning, *Memory Power For Exams*, Cliffs Notes, 1983.

Wade E. Cutler, *Triple Your Reading Speed*, Simon & Schuster, 1988.

James Deese and Stewart H. Hulse, *The Psychology Of Learning*, McGraw-Hill, 1967.

Michael J. McCarthy, *Mastering the Information Age*, Jeremy P. Tarcher, Inc., 1990.

Sheila Ostrander and Lynn Schroeder, *Super-Learning*, Delta, 1979.

P. David Pearson and Dale D. Johnson, *Teaching Reading Comprehension*, Holt Rinehart and Winston, 1974.

Mouni Sadhu, *Concentration: A Guide To Mental Mastery*, Wilshire Company, 1972.

————, *Theurgy, The Art Of Effective Worship*, George Allen & Unwin Ltd., 1965.

Nila Banton Smith, *Speed Reading Made Easy*, Warner Books, 1963.

Frank Stanley, *Remember Everything You Read*, Random House, 1990.

James S. Trefil, *The Moment Of Creation: Big Bang Physics From Before The First Millisecond To The Present Universe*, Macmillan, 1983.

Richard T. Vacca and Jo Anne L. Vacca, *Content Area Reading*, Little Brown, 1986.

Robert Keith Wallace and Herbert Benson, "The Physiology Of Meditation," *Scientific American*, February, 1972.

Paul B. Weisz, *The Science Of Biology*, McGraw-Hill, 1967.

Fred Alan Wolf, *Taking The Quantum Leap*, Harper & Row, 1981.

Gary Zukav, *The Dancing Wu Li Masters: An Overview Of The New Physics*, Bantam Books, 1984.

APPENDIX ONE

Answers to Unit One Sample Examination

1. *c*
2. *b*
3. *d*
4. *a*
5. *b*
6. *a*
7. *c*
8. *a*
9. *c*
10. *c*

11. *music*
12. *Bohr*
13. *continuous*
14. *Quanta*
15. *Uranus, Neptune, Pluto*
16. *string*
17. *singing angels*
18. *electrons*
19. *Newton*
20. *auditorium seats*

Answers to Unit Two Sample Examination

1. *b*
2. *a*
3. *b*
4. *a*

5. *b*
6. *b*
7. *a*
8. *d*

9. *c*
10. *a*
11. *virtual photon*
12. *slows*
13. *atomic*
14. *wave*

15. *particle*
16. *psychotronic*
17. *Bell*
18. *changes*
19. *186,000*
20. *Strategic Defense*

Answers to Unit Three Sample Examination

1. *c*
2. *d*
3. *c*
4. *a*
5. *a*
6. *c*
7. *c*
8. *d*
9. *a*
10. *b*

11. *super*
12. *scalar*
13. *Einstein*
14. *Tesla*
15. *Priore*
16. *quarks*
17. *two*
18. *televisions, fluorescent lights*
19. *electricity*
20. *controversial*

APPENDIX TWO

Summary of Techniques for Increasing Reading Speed

HOW TO DETERMINE YOUR READING SPEED

Steps

1. Set an alarm clock so that it rings after one minute.
2. Read at your comprehension rate until the alarm clock rings.
3. Count the number of words in five typical lines. Be careful to count lines and not sentences. Do not count punctuation marks as words.
4. Round off the number of words to the nearest number divisible by five.
5. Divide your total by five, and write down your answer. This will give you the average number of words per line.
6. Count the number of lines on a typical page. Write down this number.

7. Multiply the number of words on an average line by the average number of lines per page. This will give you the average number of words per page.

8. Divide this number by four to determine the average number of words on a quarter page.

9. Measure the amount you read to the nearest quarter page, and multiply by the number of words per page.

PICKING A HAND AND FOCAL POINT

1. Begin this exercise using your left hand.

2. Set an alarm clock so that it rings after one minute.

3. Use your pointer finger and middle finger to move your eyes across the line of text.

4. During the first minute, fix your eyes behind your fingers.

5. During the second minute, fix your eyes in front of your fingers.

6. During the third minute, fix your eyes above your fingers.

7. For the next three minutes, repeat these steps using your right hand.

8. Decide which hand feels more comfortable, and where you want to focus your eyes.

9. Set an alarm clock so that it rings after five minutes.

10. Use your preferred hand and eye positions for five minutes, and continue practicing in Appendix Two.

11. Remember to use your free hand to keep the book from snapping shut.

Left-Hand Page-Turning Technique

1. Use your left hand to start reading at the upper left-hand corner of this book's first page.
2. As your left hand begins to move down the page, slide your right hand under the corner of the top of the right page.
3. Grasp the edge of the right page, and wait until your left hand reaches the bottom of the right page.
4. Quickly flip over the page and continue reading the next page with your left hand.
5. Remember to use your right hand to keep the book from snapping shut while reading.
6. Repeat steps 1 through 4 until you have completed ten pages.

Right-Hand Page-Turning Technique

1. Use your right hand to start reading at the upper left-hand corner of this book's first page.
2. When you reach the bottom of the left page, move your right hand to the top of the right page.
3. As you complete the right page, quickly slide your right hand up to the corner of the page and flip it over.
4. Remember to use your left hand to keep the book from snapping shut while reading.

Tips for Backward Reading

1. You can vary your reading speed by moving your hand faster or slower.

2. Tracing narrow loops through text gives the best comprehension, but slows down your reading speed.
3. Tracing wide loops through text gives the best reading speed, but can reduce the comprehension of text.
4. You can form both wide and narrow loops to get the optimum combination of speed and comprehension.
5. If you find it frustrating to read backward, discontinue your efforts until you master forward reading at high speed.

HOW TO READ MULTIPLE LINES OF TEXT

1. Read Sample Unit Two, which starts on page 218.
2. Use an alarm clock to time your three-minute exercises.
3. Read one line of text at your best comprehension rate for three minutes.
4. Read two lines of text at a time for three minutes. For the duration of this exercise, it is not important that you comprehend the text.
5. Read four lines of text at a time for three minutes.
6. Read a paragraph at a time for three minutes.

SCRIPT FOR TAPE

Record the words on each numbered line onto a blank tape. Follow the instructions given in italics, but do not record them onto your tape.

1. "Start reading one line of text at your best comprehension rate."
   Wait for your alarm clock to ring after three minutes.
2. "Stop."

3. "Start reading two lines of text at a time."
   Wait for your alarm clock to ring after three minutes.
4. "Stop."
5. "Start reading four lines of text at a time."
   Wait for your alarm clock to ring after three minutes.
6. "Start reading a paragraph at a time."
7. "Stop."

HOW TO READ AT A FASTER RATE

Steps

1. Continue reading Sample Unit Two, which begins on page 218.
2. Use an alarm clock to time your three-minute exercises.
3. Complete one page every five seconds. Continue reading for three minutes. Make certain you complete each page in exactly five seconds. Do not concern yourself with comprehension during this exercise.
4. Complete one page every two seconds. Continue reading for three minutes.

SCRIPT FOR TAPE

Record the words on each numbered line onto a blank tape. Follow the instructions given in italics, but do not record them onto your tape.

1. "Start reading one page every five seconds."
   Wait for your alarm clock to ring after three minutes.
2. "Stop."
3. "Start reading one page every two seconds."
   Wait for your alarm clock to ring after three minutes.
4. "Stop."

SPEED MASTERY EXERCISE ONE
(GO TO SAMPLE UNIT THREE, ON PAGE 224)

1. Read for one minute at your best comprehension rate.
2. During the second minute, continue reading new material. Use a rate that is double your first minute's speed. Do not concern yourself with comprehension during this minute.
3. During the third minute, continue reading new material. Use a rate that is triple your first minute's speed. Do not concern yourself with comprehension during this minute.
4. During the fourth minute, continue reading new material at your best comprehension rate.
5. Repeat this entire exercise three more times.

SCRIPT FOR TAPE

Record the words on each numbered line onto a blank tape. Follow the instructions given in italics, but do not record them onto your tape. To time the exercise, set an alarm clock so that it rings after one minute.

1. "Start reading at your comprehension rate for one minute."
   Wait for your alarm clock to ring after one minute.
2. "Start reading at double your reading rate for one minute."
   Wait for your alarm clock to ring after one minute.
3. "Start reading at triple your reading rate for one minute."
   Wait for your alarm clock to ring after one minute.

4. "Start reading at your best comprehension rate for one minute."
This exercise should be repeated four times. Record steps 1 through 4 three more times on your tape before beginning the exercise.

IMPORTANT TIPS FOR HIGH-SPEED READING

1. After completing the first minute of the exercise, quickly mark off the pages in your text that you need to reach at the end of the second and third minutes.
2. During the second minute, do not worry about comprehension; instead, focus solely upon completing your goal on time.
3. During the second minute, you must complete as many pages in the first 30 seconds as you completed during the first minute. During the second 30 seconds, you should again complete as many pages as you read in the first minute. For example, if you read one page during the first minute, you should read two pages during the second minute. If you read 1.5 pages during the first minute, then you should read three pages during the second minute. Make certain you keep pace with the timing tape.
4. During the third minute, you must complete as many pages in each 20-second interval as you completed during the first minute. For example, if you read one page during the first minute, you should read three pages during the third minute. If you read 1.5 pages during the first minute, then you should read 4.5

pages during the third minute. Make certain you keep pace with the timing tape.

5. Many individuals who have difficulty reading backward find they can use backward reading to increase their speed during the second and third minutes of this exercise. Since comprehension is not important during these minutes, it is a wonderful opportunity to master backward-reading skills. Many of these individuals claim that practicing backward reading during these minutes eventually leads to successfully reading backward with comprehension.

6. For peak results, every few days deliberately increase your top speed by a quarter of a page. If you find yourself not comprehending anything, then return to your previous rate. Most likely, you will find that you can read much faster with comprehension than you believed. Usually, it is the fear of missing information that slows you down, rather than your ability to comprehend at higher speeds. This exercise will help you conquer that fear so you can achieve your maximum reading speed.

SPEED MASTERY TECHNIQUE TWO

1. Read at your comprehension rate for one minute.

2. Read for one minute at double your reading rate. Slow down to comprehend the topic sentences. Maintain your average rate by increasing your speed in the rest of the paragraphs.

3. Read for one minute at triple your reading rate. Slow down to read the topic sentences. Maintain your average rate by increasing your speed in the rest of the paragraphs.

4. Remember to maintain your average reading rate during the second and third minutes. You have not changed the total reading time, instead, you vary where your eye focuses in the text. As a result you obtain the maximum information in the shortest possible time.

SCHEMATIC SPEED INCREASING TECHNIQUE

1. Choose a nonfiction book on a familiar subject.
2. Using your hand motions, begin reading the book at your highest comprehension rate.
3. When you encounter familiar information, increase your reading speed to your double or triple reading rate.
4. Slow down to read the topic sentences, verbs, and nouns that provide the schema of the material.
5. When you encounter new information, once again slow down your reading speed to your highest comprehension rate.
6. Continue practicing this technique in three chapters of your book.
7. For peak performance, continue using this exercise in a different book each day.

Appendix Pavlov
Pavlov's Dog

Who would have thought that a dog drooling over its food would lead to one of the most important psychological discoveries in history? In 1902, Pavlov, a Russian Psychologist began a series of experiments that revolutionized our understanding of learning. His most famous experiments used a hungry dog.

Pavlov knew that a dog salivates when fed, and attempted to condition the animal to droll upon hearing a ringing bell. Pavlov rang a bell, just before feeding the dog. Soon, the animal began to associate the ringing of the bell with the start of a meal. Pavlov noted that eventually, the dog drooled upon hearing the bell, even if no food was presented. Apparently the dog transferred its instinctive reaction to food to the ringing of the bell. Pavlov called this form of learning classical conditioning.

Classical conditioning introduced four new vocabulary words into the language of the Psychologist. One of these words is *Unconditioned Stimulus (UCS)*. An unconditioned stimulus is any stimulus that can produce a response in an organism without any training. The drooling to food exhibited by the dog was not learned, it was an instinctive reaction.

Another Psychological term derived from this classical conditioning experiment is the *Unconditioned Response (UCR)*. The UCR is a response that consistently is seen each time the unconditioned stimulus is presented. In this experiment, the dog drooled each time food was presented to it. Drooling was the unconditioned response.

The *Conditioned Stimulus (CS)* is the new stimulus that an organism responds to following classical learning. Under normal conditions a dog does not drool when hearing a bell. After conditioning, Pavlov's dog responded to the ringing of the bell by drooling. As a result of the experiment, the bell now had the power to elicit the salivation response in the dog.

The *Conditioned Response (CS)* is the reaction an organism has to the conditioned stimulus. In this experiment, the presentation of the ringing bell was the conditioned stimulus.

Although simple in concept, Pavlov's work was an important advancement for Psychologists. There isn't a branch in modern psychology untouched by Pavlov's discovery of classical conditioning.